Favorite BULLETIN BOARDS

FROM

Classroom Beautiful®

Classroom Beautiful®, a bulletin board club from The Education Center, Inc., features ready-to-use, seasonal and holiday bulletin board sets. To create this book, we selected 60 of the best ideas from the *Classroom Beautiful®* program especially for teachers who enjoy making their own bulletin boards.

We've provided patterns and easy-to-follow instructions for you and your students to create colorful, eye-catching bulletin boards for every month of the year. Display student work, highlight a skill, or welcome each new season! With this idea-packed resource, your classroom can be *Classroom Beautiful®!*

Editors
Kathy Wolf, Amanda Wheeler

Copy Editors
Debbie Blaylock, Carol Rawleigh

Artists
Jennifer T. Bennett, Cathie Carter, Teresa Davidson
Susan Hodnett, Sherry Neidigh, Irene Wareham
Terri Anderson Lawson, Charlene Shidisky

Cover Designer
Jennifer T. Bennett

www.themailbox.com

©1994 by THE EDUCATION CENTER, INC.
All rights reserved.
ISBN #1-56234-104-9

Manufactured in the United States

10 9 8 7 6

Table Of Contents

Your class will flip this fall for a bulletin board that emphasizes teamwork! Cover your bulletin board with green background paper. Enlarge, color, and cut out the patterns on pages 45–47. Arrange the characters on the board as shown and add the title. Duplicate the leaf pattern below on red, yellow, tan, and orange construction paper for students to cut out. Label each leaf cutout with a student name or a class goal. Add the leaves to the board as shown or make a leaf border.

Leaf Pattern

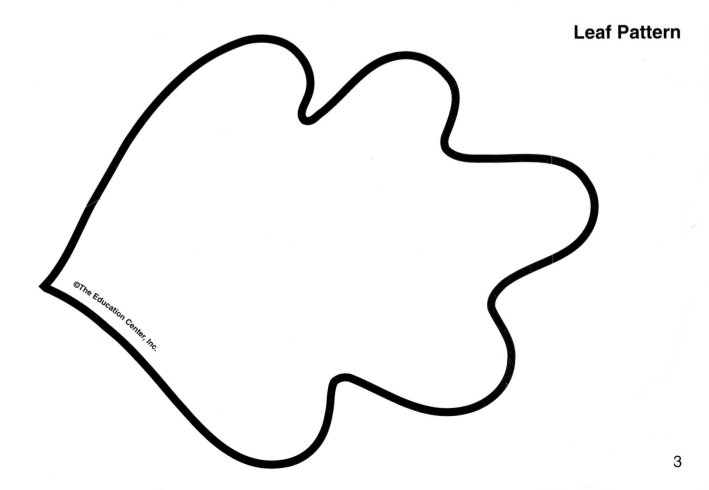

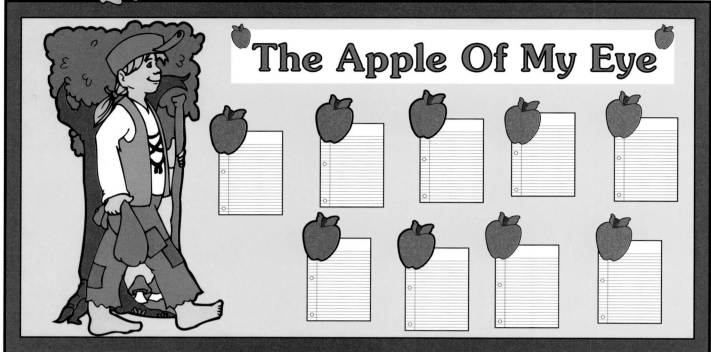

Celebrate Johnny Appleseed's birthday on September 26 with a bushel of apple activities. Use Johnny to introduce a unit on tall tales or pioneers. Cover your bulletin board with yellow background paper. Enlarge, color, and cut out the patterns on pages 47 and 48. Duplicate, color, and cut out the apple patterns. Use the apple cutouts to accent student papers, or program the apples with apple-related tasks, math problems, or story starters.

Deputize your students to help this ropin' sheriff round up some good work. Cover your bulletin board with red background paper. Enlarge and color the sheriff on page 49. Mount him on the board with a yarn lasso and a "Wanted" title. Lasso Well-Mannered Wranglers; Rootin'-Tootin' Readers; Star Spellers; Math Mavericks; or Handwriting Honchos. Duplicate the badge on page 49 on yellow construction paper. Label each star cutout with a student name. Pin the stars around the board for a border of badges. As students reach class goals or exhibit good behavior, pin their badges within the lasso.

We're A Team!

Give a cheer for teamwork with this bulletin-board banner. Cover your board with dark blue or yellow background paper. Enlarge, color, and cut out the characters on pages 50 and 51. Mount them so that they peek over and hold the banner. Duplicate the award below for students who have shown progress or completed a cooperative-learning activity.

"Give A Cheer!"

Welcome students, parents, and staff back to school with worms and apples. Cover your board with dark blue or yellow background paper. Enlarge, color, and cut out the characters on page 52. Mount them on your bulletin board or on your classroom door with a welcome message. Duplicate the apple patterns below to color and cut out. Label an apple cutout for each child in your class and add it to the board.

Apple Patterns

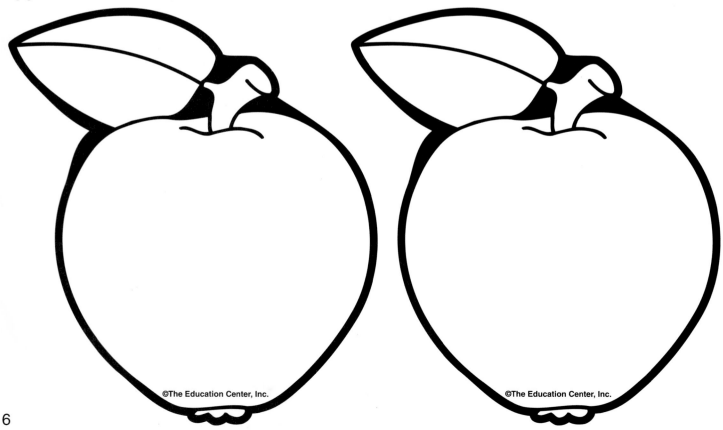

©The Education Center, Inc.   ©The Education Center, Inc.

All aboard the School Express! Cover your board with light blue or yellow background paper. Enlarge, color, and cut out the train cars on pages 53 and 54. Label the cars with color words, letters of the alphabet, or numerals for students to sequence. Mount the cars on your bulletin board or above your chalkboard. Write a title on a puff of smoke cut from white construction paper. Mount the smoke cutouts as shown. For a variation, write book titles on the cars and change the title to "Reading Express."

Cover your board with light blue or yellow background paper. Enlarge, color, and cut out the elephant on page 55. Duplicate the balloon patterns on pastel-colored construction paper. Cut out a balloon for each child. Label each balloon with the child's name and birth date. Mount the elephant and balloons as shown. Attach a string to each balloon and tie the strings together at the elephant's trunk.

Juggling clowns wish students "Happy Birthday!" Cover your board with light blue or yellow background paper. Enlarge, color, and cut out the clowns on pages 56 and 57. Cut balls from colored construction paper. Label each ball with the child's name and birth date. Mount the clowns and balls as shown. Add the title and a polka-dot border if desired.

These tugboats help you get class chores done. Enlarge, color, and cut out the tugboat and pelican patterns on page 58. Label each tugboat with a classroom job. Cut puffs of smoke from white construction paper. Label a smoke cutout for each child. Place the puffs of smoke above the tugboats to designate classroom helpers each week. To make a welcome-back-to-school board, change the title to "Welcome Aboard!" or "Sail Into First Grade!"

Squirrels scurry to get their jobs done. Enlarge, color, and cut out the squirrels and the treehouse on pages 59 and 60. Label each squirrel hole with a classroom job. Duplicate the patterns below and cut out acorns from tan construction paper. Label an acorn for each child. Place the acorns in the tree holes to show classroom helpers. Duplicate the desktags for students to write their names on and then color.

Acorn Patterns

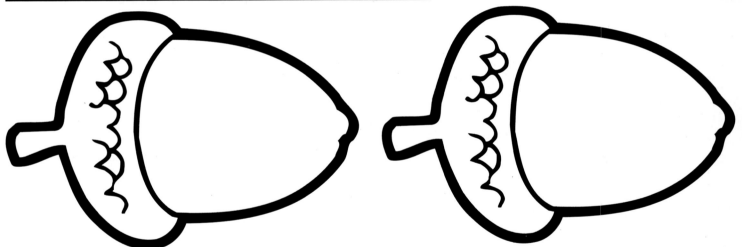

Helper's Desktag

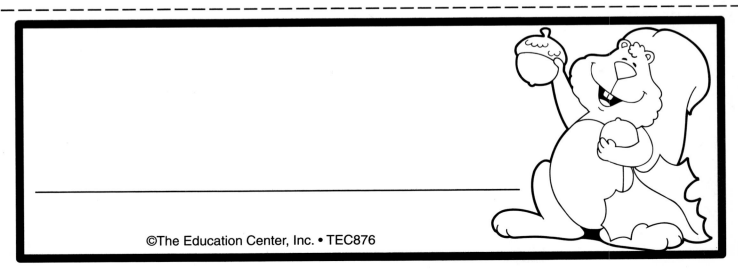

9

These teddy bears cheer for good work! Enlarge, color, and cut out the patterns on pages 61 and 62. Mount the cheerleaders on the board with the title "Go, Team, Go!" Display student papers or photos. Change the title to "Hip, Hip, Hooray For Reading!" or "Give A Cheer For Our Math Stars!"

This fire fighter and Dalmatian help you teach fire safety rules during Fire Prevention Week in October. Cover your bulletin board with dark blue background paper. Enlarge, color, and duplicate the patterns on pages 63 and 64. Label fire-hydrant cutouts or a poster with fire safety rules. Add a border of Dalmatian spots if desired.

In 1492, Columbus sailed the ocean blue. Encourage your students to set sail on new adventures with Columbus. Enlarge, color, and cut out the patterns on pages 65 and 66. Mount Columbus with his three ships on the board. Add a title such as "Set Sail For Spelling!" or "Thanks To Columbus!" Students can use the globe pattern below to make a border.

Globe Pattern

These raccoon trick-or-treaters are ready for a safe Halloween. Cover your board with orange or purple background paper. Enlarge, color, and cut out the raccoon patterns on pages 67–69. Add the title "Have A Safe Halloween!" and Halloween safety tips if you wish. Duplicate the mask pattern on page 13 for students to color and cut out. Use the masks to make a border.

Five little kittens peeking from pumpkins create a Halloween greeting! Enlarge, color, and cut out the patterns on pages 69–71. Have each child cut out a pumpkin from orange construction paper to add to the display. Add features cut from black construction paper to make a pumpkin patch full of jack-o'-lanterns. Add a title such as "Happy Halloween!" or "Peek-A-Boo!"

Friendly ghosts peek out of a haunted house and over your bulletin board to view "boo-tiful" work! Enlarge, color, and cut out the patterns on pages 72 and 73. Have students make bat cutouts to accent their papers. See page 14 for a bat pattern.

Mask Pattern
Use with "Have A Safe Halloween!" on page 12.

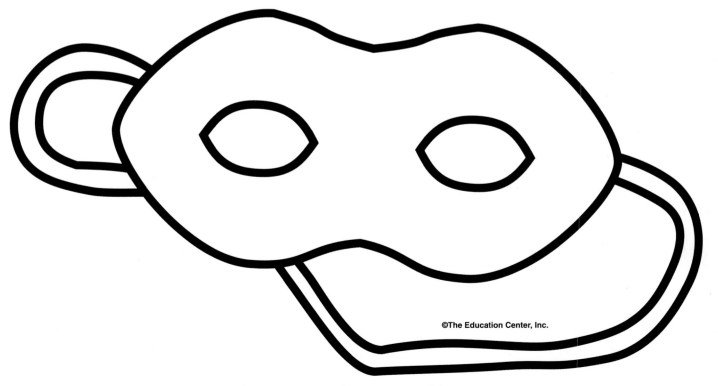

©The Education Center, Inc.

Little Witch is riding high to wish everyone a happy Halloween! Enlarge, color, and cut out the witch pattern on page 74. Place her broomstick so that she hovers over the bulletin board. Duplicate the pumpkin pattern on page 73 and the bat pattern below for students to cut out and color. Use the pumpkins and bats to accent students' good work.

Bat Pattern

14

Students can make pumpkins to add to Mr. Scarecrow's pumpkin patch. Cover your bulletin board with dark blue background paper. Enlarge, color, and duplicate the patterns on pages 75 and 76. Have students finger-paint and cut out pumpkins. Enlarge, color, and duplicate the crow patterns below to make a title strip as shown.

Crow Patterns

©The Education Center, Inc.

©The Education Center, Inc.

Build excitement for National Children's Book Week in November with a construction-site bulletin board. Students can add tool cutouts labeled with favorite titles and authors. Cover your board with yellow construction paper. Enlarge, color, and cut out the characters on pages 77–79. Duplicate the tool patterns on white paper for students to color and cut out. Use the tool cutouts for a border.

Get children hooked on books during National Library Week in April with a reading incentive board. Cover your board with light blue background paper. Enlarge, color, and cut out the patterns on pages 80 and 81. Assemble the board as shown with the waves bowed out. Staple a length of string to the fishing pole and attach a paper clip. Clip a book cover to the line. Duplicate the book jacket pattern on page 81. Have students decorate the book jackets with favorite titles and pin them below the waves. Duplicate the bookmarks on page 82 on colored construction paper. Have each student color a book on his bookmark each time he reads a book.

16

Cover your board with dark blue or black background paper. Enlarge, color, and cut out the planets, astronauts, and space shuttle patterns on pages 83–86. Mount the astronauts on the board as shown. Attach a length of thick yarn to each astronaut and then the shuttle. Duplicate the star patterns below on yellow construction paper for students to cut out and label with book titles. To vary the use of this board, label star cutouts with facts about the solar system. Change the title to "Read About The Solar System."

Star Patterns

Sharing The Harvest!

Use this bulletin board to introduce the story of the first Thanksgiving and discuss how the Pilgrims and Native Americans shared the harvest. Cover your bulletin board with yellow background paper. Enlarge, color, and cut out the patterns on pages 87–89. Duplicate the cornucopia pattern below on white paper for students to color and cut out. Ask students to draw or cut out pictures of foods for their cornucopias. Add these horns of plenty to the board.

Cornucopia Pattern

©The Education Center, Inc.

This gobbler greets good work with turkey talk! Enlarge, color, and cut out the turkey pattern on page 90. Duplicate the feather pattern on page 90 on colored construction paper for students to cut out and fringe. Add the feathers to the board as a border or to accent "fine-feathered" work.

Even the forest animals are sharing this Thanksgiving dinner! Cover your bulletin board with yellow background paper. Enlarge, color, and cut out the patterns on pages 91–96. Duplicate the cornucopia pattern on page 18 to begin your title strip. Duplicate the leaf pattern on page 3 on orange, red, yellow, and brown paper for students to create a border.

Winter

Santa's elves help to display gift-wrapped good work. Enlarge, color, and cut out the elves on pages 97–99. Create a title and border from holiday wrapping paper. If you wish, duplicate the holly and berries patterns on page 98 for students to color and cut out to make a border.

Teddy bears remind us that the best holiday gift is a hug! Cover your board with dark blue background paper. Enlarge, color, and cut out the teddy bears on pages 100–101. Duplicate the holiday hug award on page 21 on red construction paper to give to students. Have students cut out package shapes from wrapping paper and add gift tags that tell to whom they would give a holiday hug and why. Use wide, plaid ribbon to make a border.

Peace On Earth

Children from around the world make a holiday wish for peace on earth. Enlarge, color, and cut out the patterns on pages 102–105. Duplicate the small dove patterns on page 105 on white paper for students to make a border of white doves. Duplicate the large dove pattern on page 106 for each child. Have each student cut out the large white dove, write his thoughts for a peaceful world, and add his wishes to the display.

Award
Use with "Give A Holiday Hug!" on page 20.

Here's a holiday hug from

_____
- -
_____

Winter

Make a grand entrance for the holidays with gingerbread cookies and candy canes around your door or bulletin board. Enlarge, color, and cut out the gingerbread house on page 107. Duplicate the candy cane patterns on page 107 on white paper and the cookie patterns on page 108 on tan paper for students to decorate and cut out. Arrange the pieces around your door as shown. Duplicate the gingerbread girl and boy on page 109 on tan construction paper for students to cut out and decorate. Label each cookie with the student's name and add to the board. Or program the gingerbread children with a skill or holiday-related tasks for the students.

Candy Patterns

22

This winter, remember our feathered friends with a tree of popcorn and berries. Cover your bulletin board with light blue background paper. Use the pattern on page 112 to cut a large evergreen tree from green bulletin-board paper. Enlarge, color, and cut out the boy and girl patterns on pages 110–111. Duplicate the bird patterns on pages 113 for students to color and cut out. Add the birds to the board. Have students decorate the tree with real popcorn and berries. Create a holiday border of holly, snowflakes, or birds.

A Fine-feathered Christmas!

Award

(Name)

has done fine-feathered work in

.

That's something to chirp about!

(Teacher)

(Date)

©The Education Center, Inc. • TEC876

Encourage each student to put his best foot forward in the new year! Enlarge, color, and cut out the girl and boy joggers on pages 114 and 115. Duplicate the sneaker patterns on pages 114 and 115 on white paper for each child to color and cut out for a border. Have students write class or individual goals on sneakers and add them to the board.

These frosty fellows can lead to a discussion of winter activities or polar animals. Cover your bulletin board with light blue or white background paper. Enlarge, color, and cut out the polar bear patterns on pages 116–118. Cut out letters from dark blue paper to create a title. Have students cut out paper snowflakes for a border.

Display students' good work with frolicking winter friends. Cover your bulletin board with dark blue background paper. Enlarge, color, and cut out the patterns on pages 119–122. Duplicate the mouse patterns on page 122 for students to color and cut out to accent their papers. Add cotton batting for snow. Create the title and add a border of paper snowflakes. Duplicate the award below for students making *cool* progress.

Award

Zippin' Ahead!

_____
(student)

is making *cool* progress in

_____

Keep up the *slick* work!

_____   _____
(teacher)   (date)

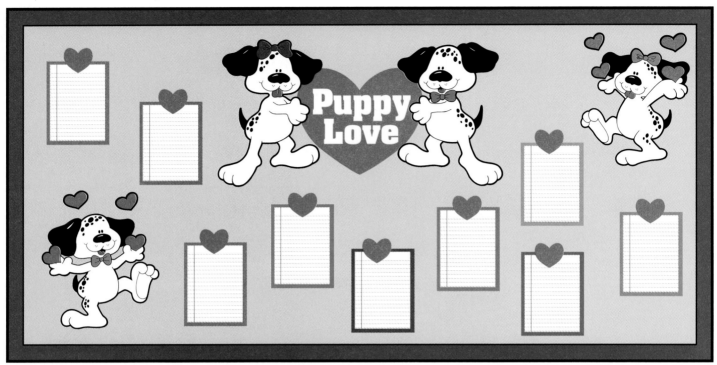

Get ready for Valentine's Day with puppies who love students' good work. Cover your board with pink or white background paper. Enlarge, color, and cut out the puppies and hearts on pages 123–125. Have students cut out and decorate red hearts with lace, ribbon, markers, and glitter to accent papers.

Tumbling teddies are head-over-heels for Valentine's Day! Cover your board with pink background paper. Enlarge, color, and cut out the teddy bear patterns on pages 126–127. Have students cut out and decorate pink and red hearts to add to the board. Add student photos if you wish.

These crazy kittens perk up your bulletin board for a "purr-fect" Valentine's Day display! Cover your board with pink or red background paper. Enlarge, color, and cut out the kittens on pages 128–130. Attach a piece of ribbon or yarn to a balloon cutout. Staple one end of the yarn to each kitten's hand. Duplicate the valentine below on pink construction paper. Punch holes as shown. Insert a lollipop for each student.

Valentine Patterns

Be Mine, Valentine!

To: _____

From: _____

Be Mine, Valentine!

To: _____

From: _____

Patriotic kids and a star-spangled border create a flag-waving display for Presidents' Day, Election Day, Flag Day, or the Fourth of July. Cover your board with light blue background paper. Enlarge, color, and cut out the patterns on pages 131–134. Create a banner from white construction paper and write the title with red and blue markers. Attach the banner to the board with long pushpins or mount the banner with Styrofoam behind it to make it stand out from the board. Duplicate the star pattern on page 133 on yellow construction paper for students to cut out. Label a star for each child or attach a student photo.

Mr. Happy Tooth and friendly Miss Floss are smiling because students are learning good dental health practices. For National Dental Health Month in February, cover your board with dark blue background paper. Enlarge, color, and cut out the patterns on pages 135 and 136. Write the title on the toothpaste cutout and label white bubbles with dental health rules. Attach the arm to the tooth and the top to the floss with brass fasteners. Punch a hole in the dental floss box and attach a piece of white yarn through the back. Assemble the board as shown. Duplicate the tooth pattern on page 135 for students to cut out to create a happy tooth border.

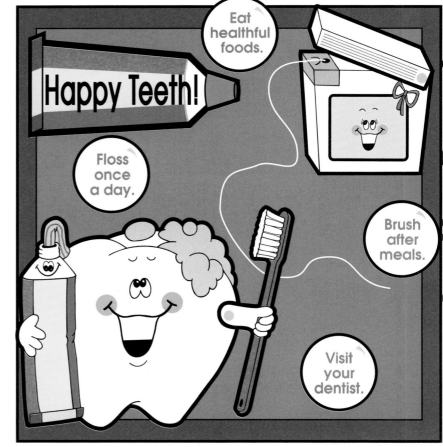

Display the Wee People with a border of shamrocks. Cover your board with blue and green background paper. Enlarge, color, and cut out the patterns on pages 137–139. Duplicate the shamrock pattern on page 141 on green paper for students to cut out and create a border.

Leprechauns teach skills with pots of gold. Enlarge, color, and cut out the leprechaun patterns on pages 140 and 141. Duplicate the pot and shamrock patterns for each child to color and cut out. Program the shamrock cutouts with Irish vocabulary and label pots with definitions to match. To vary, label pots with St. Patrick's Day tasks or math problems.

Spring

Make kite-flying days fact-finding days. Program the kites with a skill of your choice. Cover your bulletin board with light blue background paper. Cover the bottom of the board with green paper to represent grass. Enlarge, color, and cut out the boy, girl, and dog patterns on pages 142 and 143. Enlarge the patterns on page 144 on white paper for students to color and cut out several sizes of kites and kite tails. Program the kites with answers and the kite tails with math problems to match. Duplicate the award below to give to students who complete their work with flying colors.

Awards

You came through with flying colors!

_____ (teacher)

_____ (date)

©The Education Center, Inc. • TEC876

30

Create a classroom blooming with colorful student-made flowers. Cover your bulletin board with light blue background paper. Enlarge, color, and cut out the patterns on pages 145 and 146. Assemble the flower cart and title canopy as shown, bowing the canopy out for a three-dimensional effect. Duplicate the wooden shoe or tulip pattern below to make a border if desired.

Wooden Shoe And Tulip Patterns

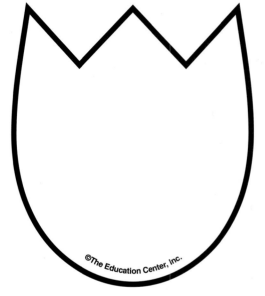

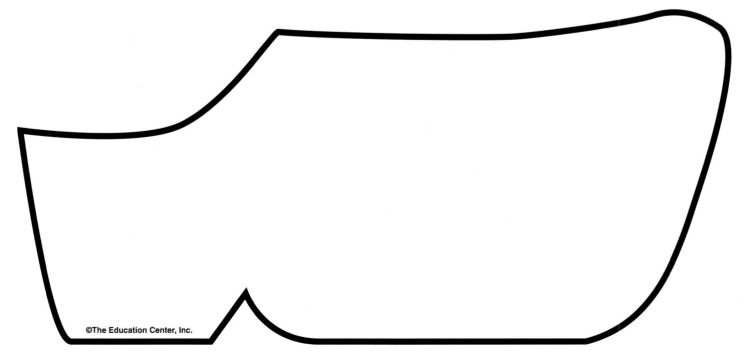

Garden Bunnies

While bunnies are busy picking vegetables from the garden, your children will be picking math problems. Cover your bulletin board with green or yellow background paper. Enlarge, color, and cut out the bunny patterns on pages 147 and 148. Duplicate the carrot patterns below on orange paper. Program the carrot cutouts with addition or multiplication facts. Program carrot tops with answers for students to match. Have students cut out carrots to make a border if you wish.

Carrot Pattern

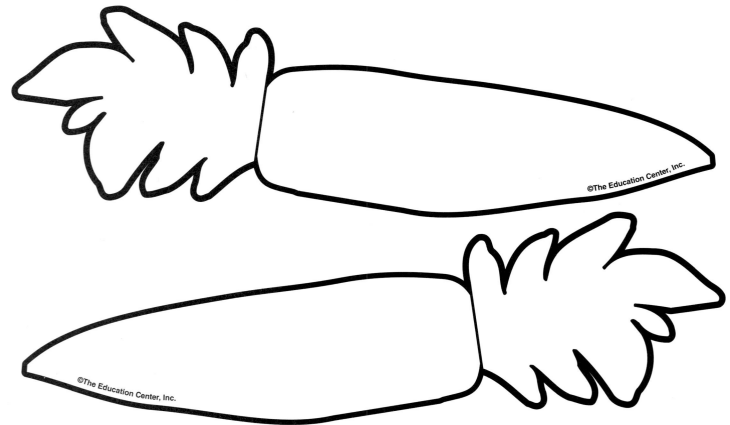

©The Education Center, Inc.

©The Education Center, Inc.

©The Education Center, Inc. • TEC876

Rainy weather is just ducky for a spring bulletin-board theme. Cover your board with light blue background paper. Enlarge, color, and cut out the duck patterns on pages 149 and 150. Duplicate the raindrop pattern on white paper. Cut out and program raindrops with vocabulary words, math problems, or rainy day tasks. Or have students write raindrop poems to add to the board. Duplicate the umbrella pattern below on pastel construction paper for students to decorate and cut out. Add a colorful border of student-made umbrellas and a title.

Umbrella Pattern

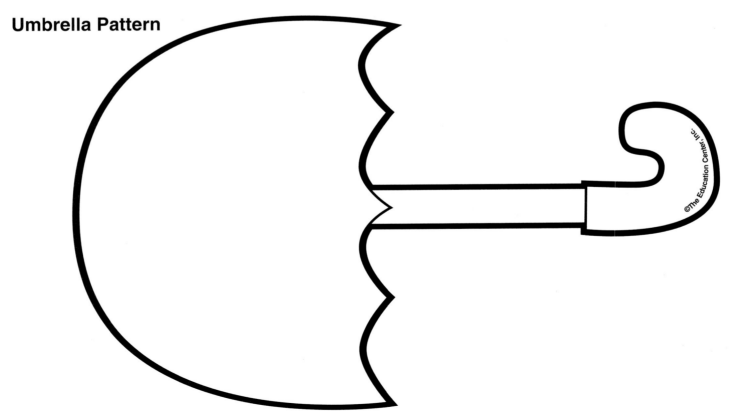

This brood of dapper chicks is ready for an Easter parade of good work. Cover your bulletin board with light blue background paper. Enlarge, color, and cut out the patterns on pages 151–153. Cut out a speech bubble from white paper and write the title inside. Use the chicks to accent student papers. Add student-created eggs for a colorful border.

Creative bunnies help your students turn out "eggs-traordinary" colored eggs for this Easter bulletin board. Cover your board with light blue or yellow background paper. Enlarge, color, and cut out the bunny patterns on pages 154–156. Have students use finger paints, markers, or watercolors to design eggs to add to the board.

This giant bunny says "Hop, hop, hooray!" for students' good work. Cover your board with light blue or yellow background paper. Enlarge, color, and cut out the rabbit pattern on page 157. Cut out a speech bubble and write the title. Have students cutout and decorate Easter eggs to accent their good work or label egg cutouts with student names, math problems, or spelling words. For a spring bulletin board, duplicate the carrot pattern on page 32 and program carrots with a skill.

Show everyone that it's been a honey of a year for your class! Cover your board with dark blue background paper. Enlarge, color, and cut out the bears and bees on pages 158 and 159. Duplicate the honey-pot pattern on page 160 for students to color and cut out. Have each child think of a memorable class event or personal accomplishment during the school year and write about it on his honey pot. Add the pots to the board with the title strip. For a working bulletin board, write classroom tasks or math problems on honey-pot cutouts and change the title to "Do A Honey Of A Job!"

Anytime

Grandfather Turtle and the turtle youngsters can help your students learn to tell time. Cover your bulletin board with yellow background paper. Enlarge, color, and cut out the patterns on pages 161–163. Duplicate the clock patterns on page 164 and program them with hours and minutes for students to match to times hidden behind each turtle. Pin the turtles to the board beside the correct clocks. Have students tell the times and lift the turtles to check.

Shape up with balancing bears. Cover your bulletin board with yellow, blue, or pink background paper. Enlarge, color, and cut out the bear patterns on pages 165 and 166. Cut out and label a triangle, oval, circle, square, and rectangle from colored construction paper. Arrange the bears and shapes on the board as shown. For alphabet matching, label cut-out shapes with upper/lowercase letters and change the title to "ABC Bears."

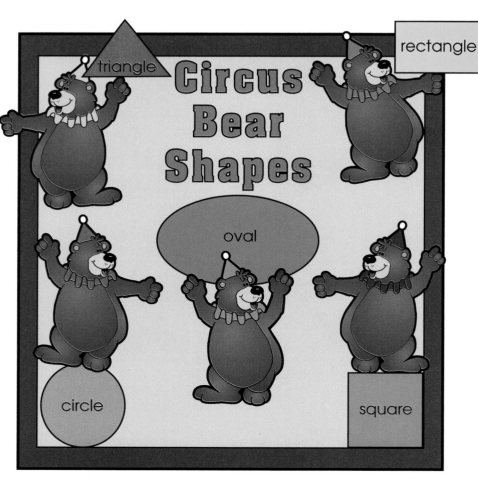

Anytime

Look What We've Cooked Up!

Your class can cook up recipes for favorite foods, good books, friendship, or good work with Chef Peekaround. Cover your bulletin board with light blue background paper. Enlarge, color, and cut out the patterns on pages 167 and 168. Arrange the pieces on the board as shown. Label cards with creative writing tasks and insert the cards in the chef's pockets. Duplicate the recipe card below for students to write their recipes. The student pulls a strip from the chef's pocket, completes the assignment, and adds his recipe card to the board.

Recipe Card Pattern

_____
name of recipe

Ingredients:

_____ _____

_____ _____

_____ _____

How To Make:

_____

_____

_____

_____

_____

Chef: _____

Anytime

Welcome spring and introduce a unit on birds with this busy birdbath bulletin board. Cover your board with light blue or yellow background paper. Enlarge, color, and cut out the patterns on pages 169 and 170. Duplicate the bird patterns on white paper for students to color and cut out. Pin the birds to the board and add labels. Display students' papers with birds. Change the title to "Something To Chirp About!"

This "dino-mite" dinosaur family admires artwork and papers by "dino-mite" kids! Cover your bulletin board with light blue background paper. Enlarge, color, and cut out the dinosaur patterns on pages 171–173. Add a title starburst.

Introduce a unit on the farm or a harvest of good work with Old MacDonald's bulletin board. Cover your board with blue and green background paper to represent the sky and earth. Enlarge, color, and cut out the patterns on pages 174–177. Arrange the cutouts on the board to show a farm scene. Have students add a border of tractor cutouts labeled with farm vocabulary, book titles, or student names.

Tractor Pattern

Anytime Under The Big Top!

Here comes the circus! Program this bulletin board to feature basic skills under a big top and extend the circus theme across the curriculum. Cover your board with dark blue background paper. Make a red-and-white striped title strip. Enlarge, color, and cut out the characters on pages 178 and 180. Cut lengths of colored yarn or ribbon to hang each trapeze artist under the big top. Assemble the board as shown. Program circus balls with problems or add circus vocabulary for students to use in creative writing. Duplicate the award below for students and display the awards on the board if desired.

Award

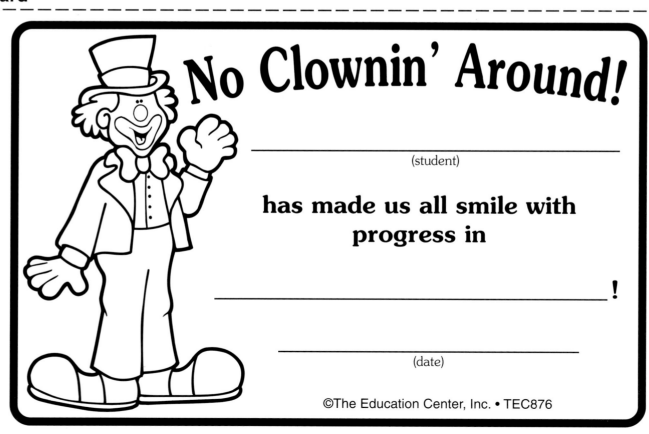

No Clownin' Around!

_____
(student)

has made us all smile with progress in

_____!

_____
(date)

The Ocean

Create an ocean bottom with student help. Cover your board with light blue background paper. Enlarge, color, and cut out the patterns on pages 181–183. Have students try one or more of the art projects below and add their sea creatures to the board.

- To make an octopus, attach eight 12-inch lengths of crepe paper to a ten-inch paper plate and add wiggle eyes.
- To make starfish, glue CheeriOs™ or Shredded Wheat™ on star-shaped construction-paper cutouts. Use a paintbrush to brush a coat of glue on the surface of the starfish. Sprinkle the crushed Shredded Wheat™ evenly on one side. Glue CheeriOs™ to the other side.
- To make an oyster shell, fold a small, white paper plate in half. Trim the folded plate to create a shell shape. Paste pink paper inside each shell half. Glue a circle of white paper inside to represent a pearl.
- To make a school of three-dimensional fish, duplicate the fish patterns on page 183 on white paper for students to color and cut out two of one fish. Decorate each shape with colored markers. Use a hole puncher to

make colored paper dots to glue on the fish for scales if desired. Staple the fish together along the edges, leaving a hole to stuff with tissue paper. After stuffing, staple the opening and mount the fish on the board with pins.

- To make seaweed, staple lengths of green crepe paper from the bottom to the top of the board. Hide fish and other sea creatures in the seaweed garden.
- To make sensational seashells, enlarge and trace shell patterns below on white construction paper. Use permanent markers to add details before painting. Cut out each shape. Using a paintbrush, brush on a coat of transparent glitter paint made from light corn syrup, food coloring, and glitter.

Shell Patterns

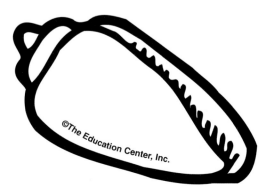

Anytime

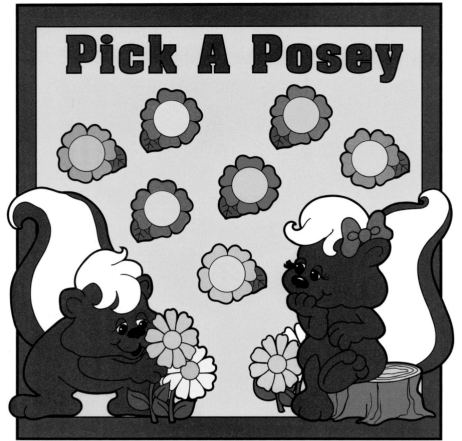

Pick A Posey

"Scent-sational" skunks are picking posies for skills practice. Cover your board with yellow background paper. Enlarge, color, and cut out the skunks on pages 184 and 185. Duplicate the flower pattern on page 184 for students to color and add to the board. Or program the flower cutouts for a matching skill.

Whooo's wise? Your students will be wiser when they complete Professor Owl's homework assignments. Enlarge the owl and owlet patterns on pages 186 and 187. Color and cut out the owls. Display student papers with the baby owls.

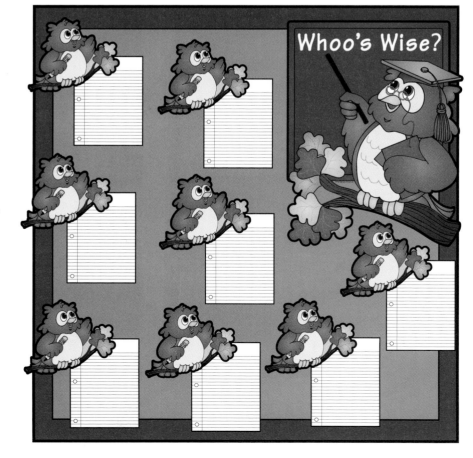

Brush Up On Facts!

Encourage students to brush up on addition, subtraction, or multiplication facts or to find the answers to science or social studies research questions. Cover your board with yellow background paper. Enlarge, color, and cut out the painters on page 188. Duplicate the paintbrush and paint-can patterns below. Program, color, and cut out the patterns. Have students match cans to brushes. Or write a question on each brush cutout and have students write the answers on the cans.

Paintbrush and Can Patterns

©The Education Center, Inc.

©The Education Center, Inc.

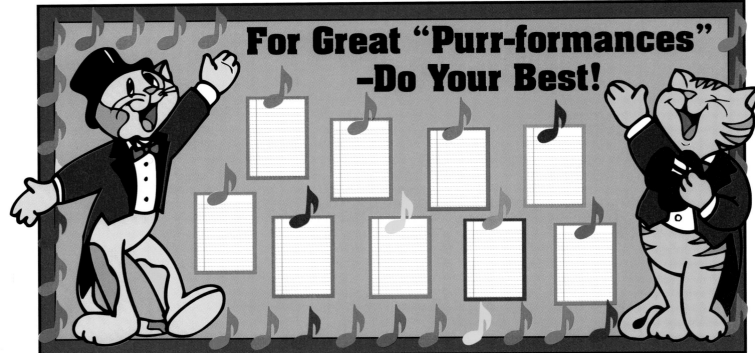

For great "purr-formances," encourage students to do their best! Cover your board with orange background paper. Enlarge, color, and cut out the top-hat cats on pages 189 and 190. Have students make a border of colorful musical notes. Place a musical note above each child's paper.

"Give it your best shot!" for math, spelling, or grammar skills. Cover your board with yellow, blue, or white background paper. Enlarge, color, and cut out the patterns on page 191 and 192. Program basketball cutouts with numerals and label the basketball backboard with an operation such as x 4 or + 9. Or label the basketballs with words to make plural, sentences to punctuate, or vocabulary words to define. Students take an answer sheet from the hoop and write their answers.

Enlarge and use with "Jump Into Fall" on page 3.

Enlarge and use with "Jump Into Fall" on page 3.

Use with "The Apple Of My Eye" on page 4.

©The Education Center, Inc.

©The Education Center, Inc.

Patterns

Enlarge and use with "The Apple Of My Eye" on page 4.

©The Education Center, Inc.

©The Education Center, Inc.

©The Education Center, Inc.

Patterns

Enlarge and use with "We're A Team!" on page 5.

©The Education Center, Inc.

©The Education Center, Inc.

©The Education Center, Inc.

©The Education Center, Inc. • TEC876

Enlarge and use with "Welcome Back!" on page 6.

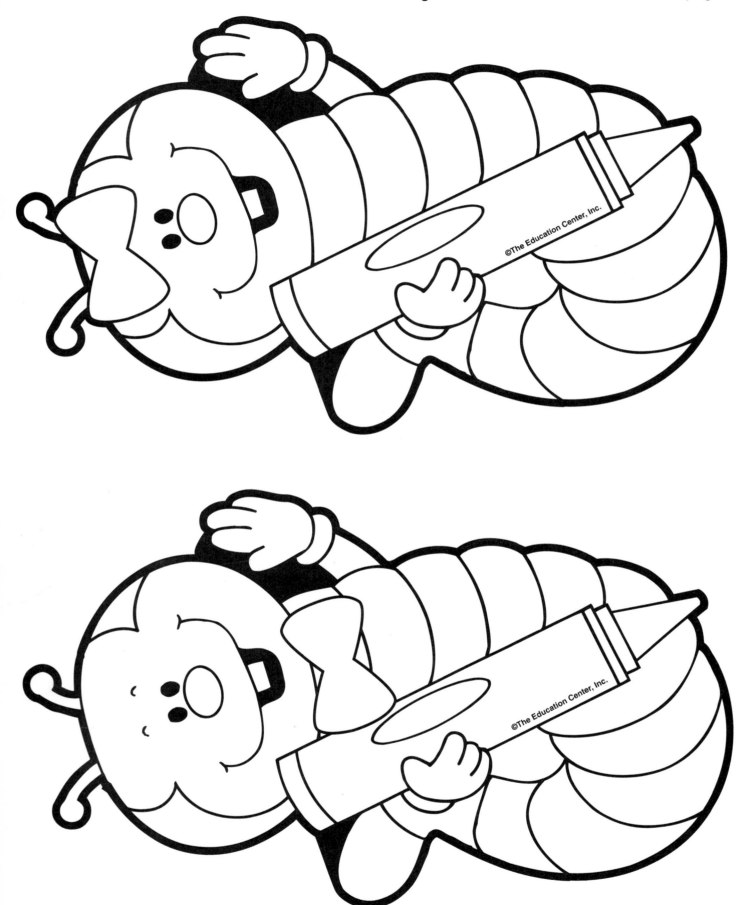

©The Education Center, Inc.

©The Education Center, Inc.

©The Education Center, Inc.

©The Education Center, Inc.

Enlarge and use with "School Express" on page 7.

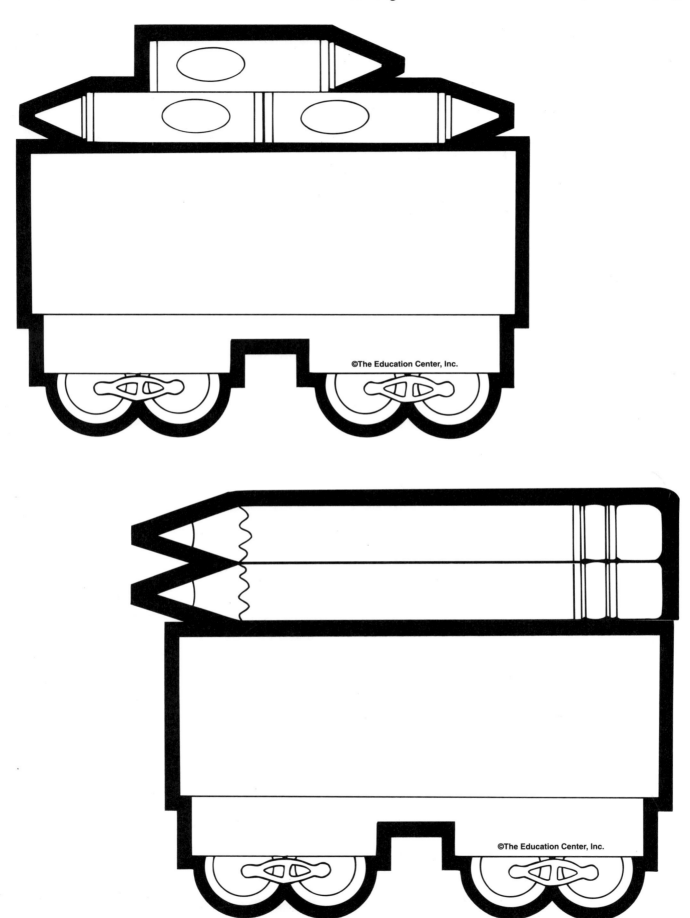

©The Education Center, Inc.

©The Education Center, Inc.

©The Education Center, Inc. • TEC876

©The Education Center, Inc.

©The Education Center, Inc.

Pattern

Enlarge and use with "Happy Birthday!" clowns on page 8.

Enlarge and use with "Happy Birthday!" clowns on page 8.

Pattern

Enlarge and use with "Little Helpers" on page 8.

©The Education Center, Inc.

Patterns

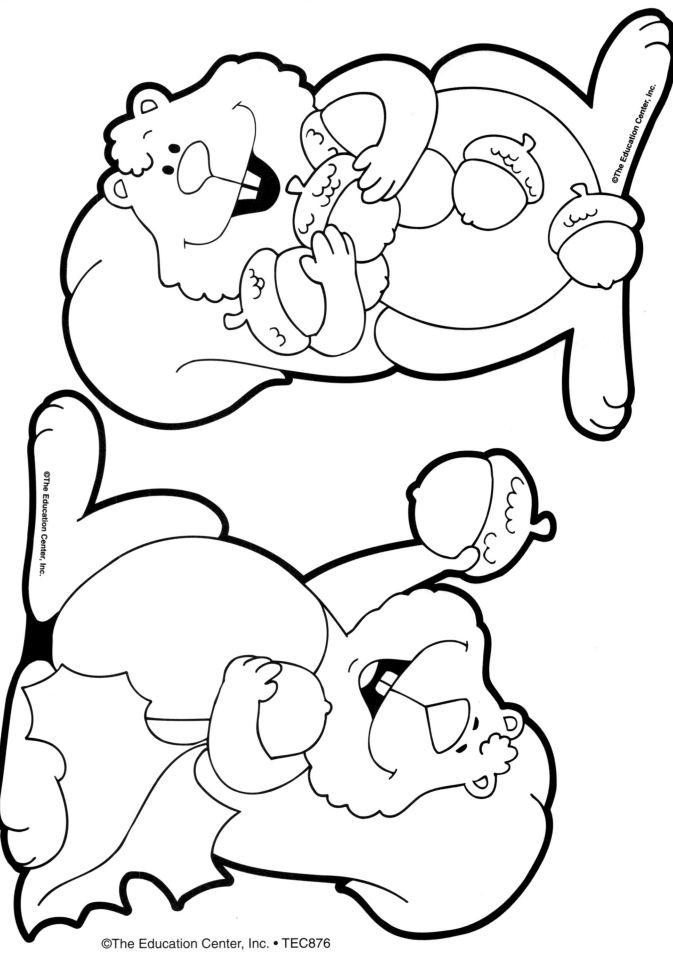

Enlarge and use with "Hurry Scurry Helpers" on page 9.

Enlarge and use with "Go, Team, Go!" on page 10.

©The Education
Center, Inc.

©The Education
Center, Inc.

©The Education
Center, Inc.

Enlarge and use with "Be Fire Safety Smart!" on page 10.

Pattern

Enlarge and use with "Be Fire Safety Smart!" on page 10.

©The Education Center, Inc.

©The Education Center, Inc.

©The Education Center, Inc. • TEC876

©The Education Center, Inc.

Patterns

Enlarge and use with "Thanks To Columbus!" on page 11.

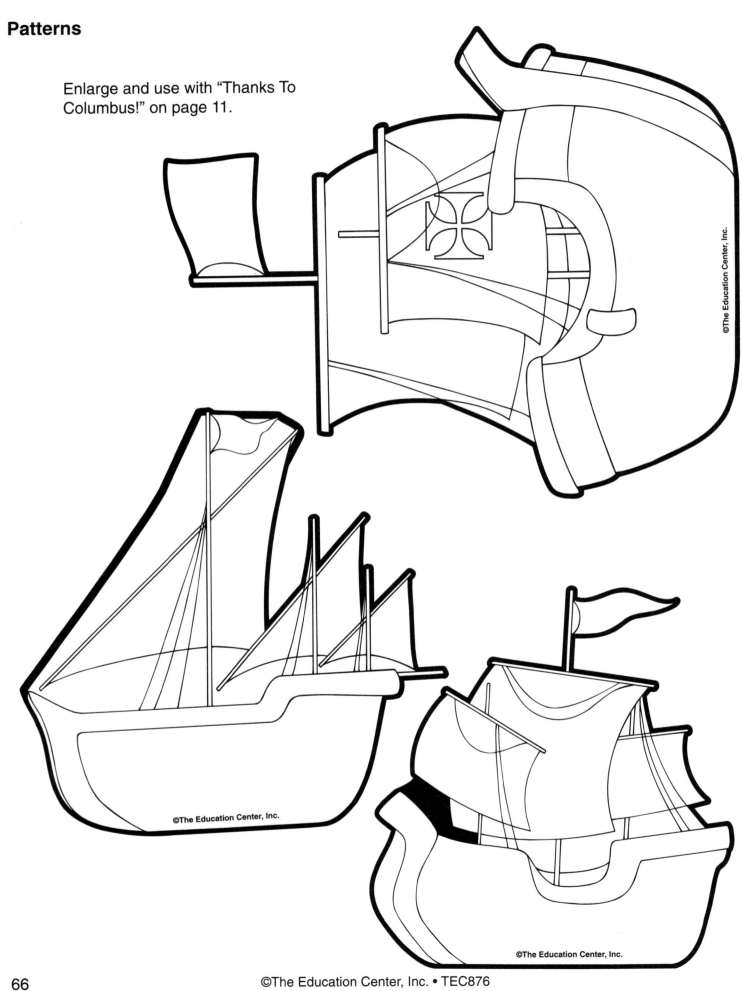

©The Education Center, Inc.

©The Education Center, Inc.

©The Education Center, Inc.

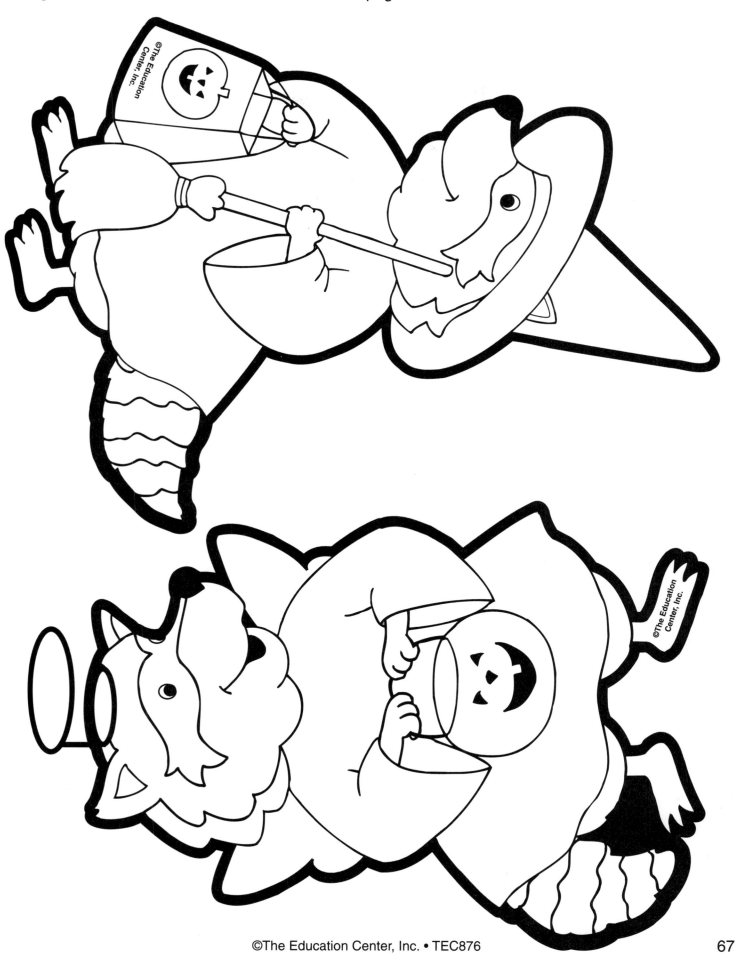

Enlarge and use with "Have A Safe Halloween!" on page 12.

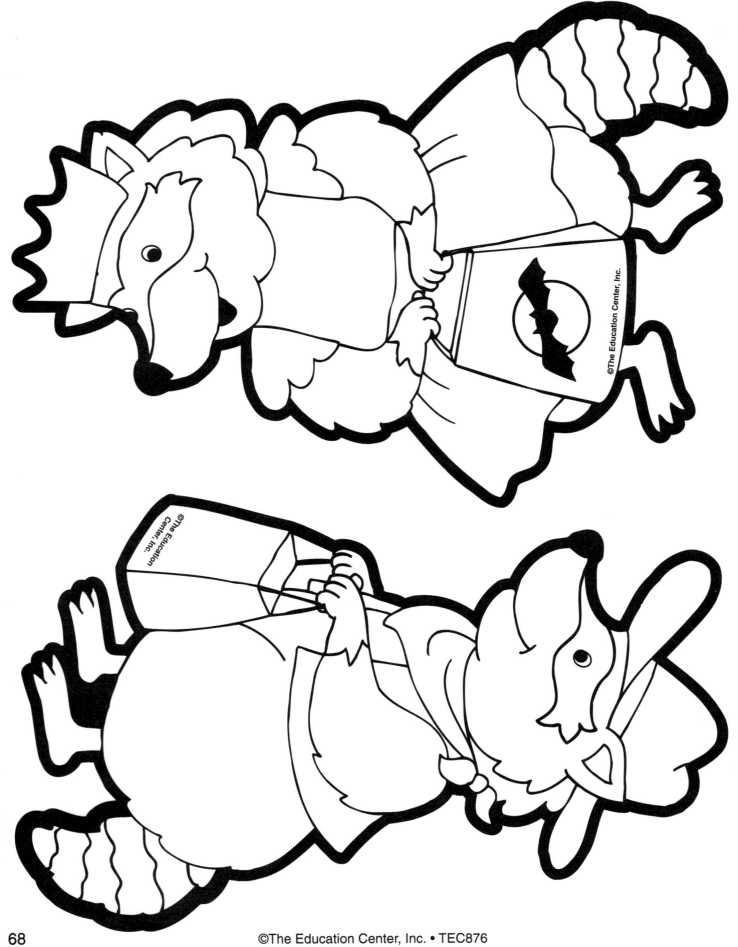

©The Education Center, Inc. • TEC876

Enlarge and use with "Have A Safe Halloween!" on page 12.

©The Education Center, Inc.

Enlarge and use with "Peek-A-Boo!" on page 12.

Enlarge and use with "Peek-A-Boo!" on page 12.

©The Education Center, Inc.

©The Education Center, Inc.

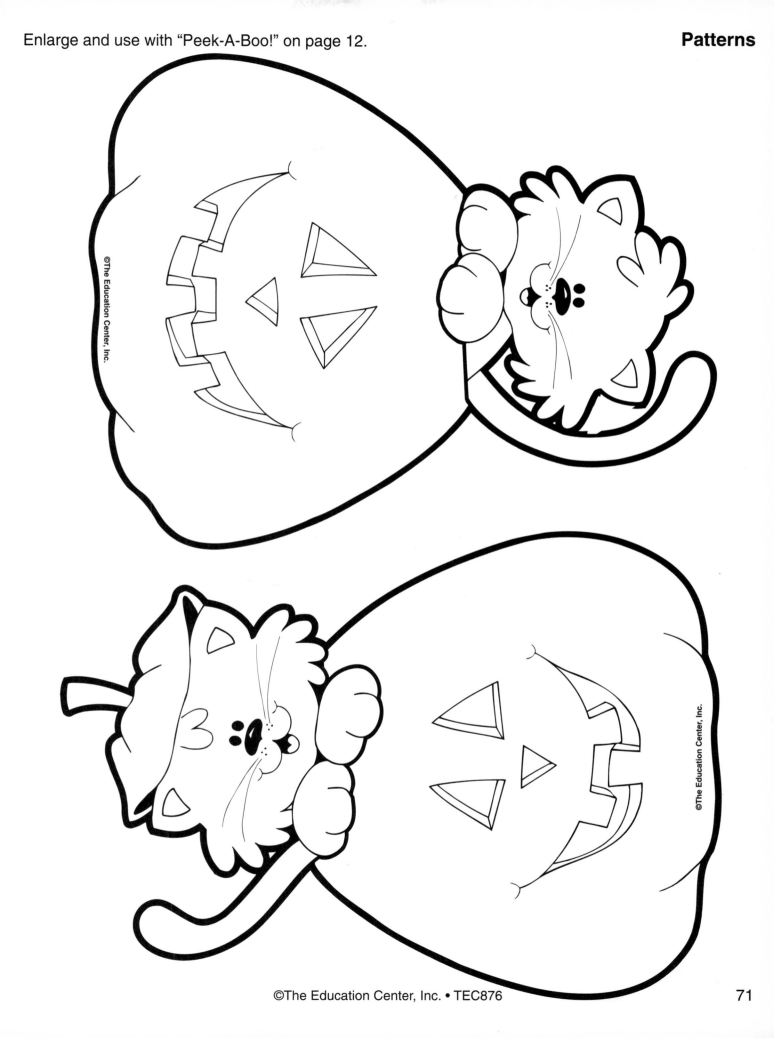

Enlarge and use with "'Boo-tiful' Work!" on page 13.

©The Education Center, Inc.

©The Education Center, Inc. • TEC876

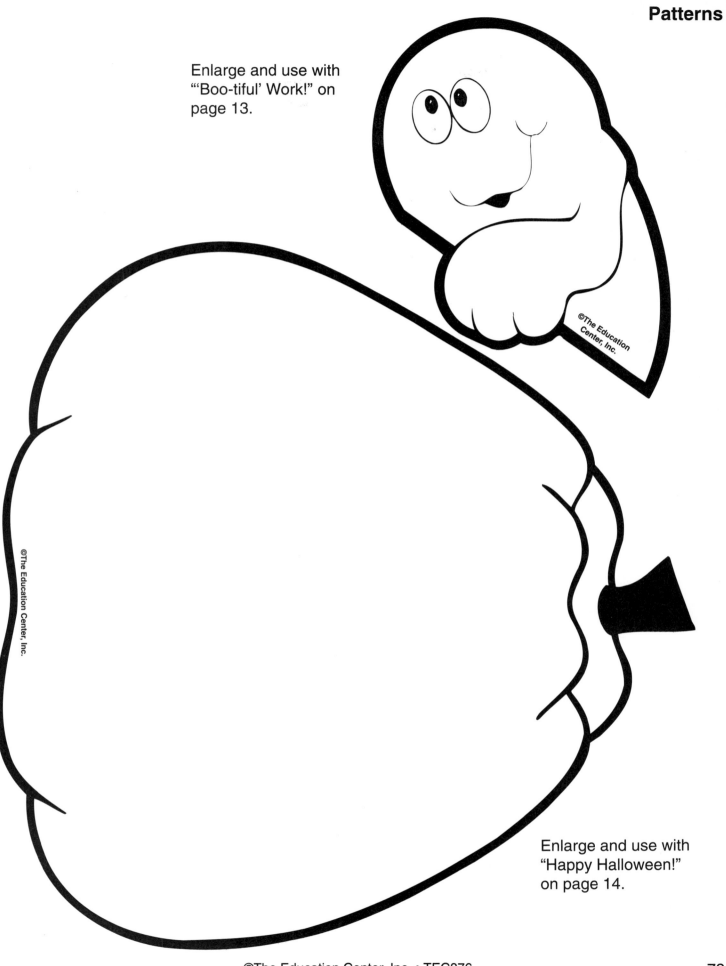

Patterns

Enlarge and use with "'Boo-tiful' Work!" on page 13.

©The Education Center, Inc.

©The Education Center, Inc.

Enlarge and use with "Happy Halloween!" on page 14.

Pattern

Enlarge and use with "Happy Halloween!" on page 14.

©The Education Center, Inc.

©The Education Center, Inc.

Enlarge and use with "Pumpkin Patch Pals" on page 15.

©The Education Center, Inc.

©The Education Center, Inc.

©The Education Center, Inc. • TEC876

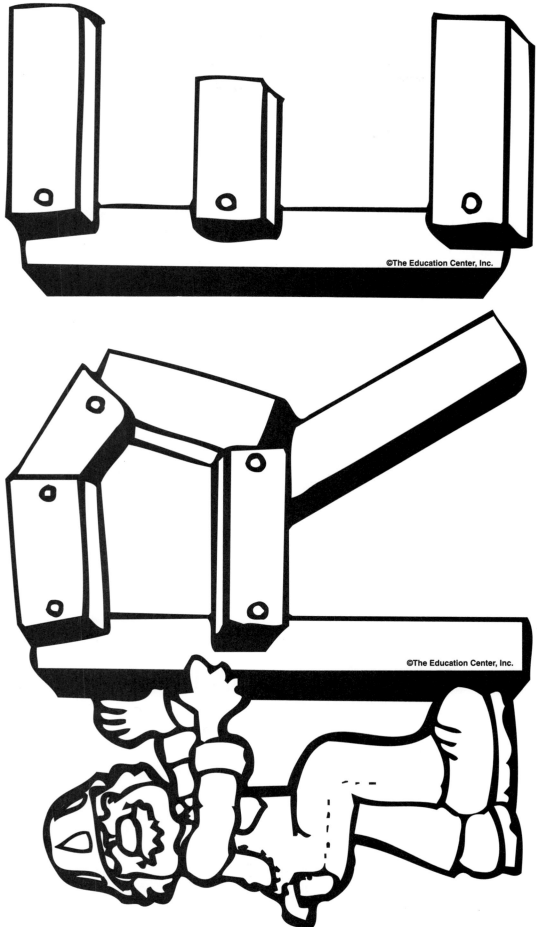

©The Education Center, Inc.

©The Education Center, Inc.

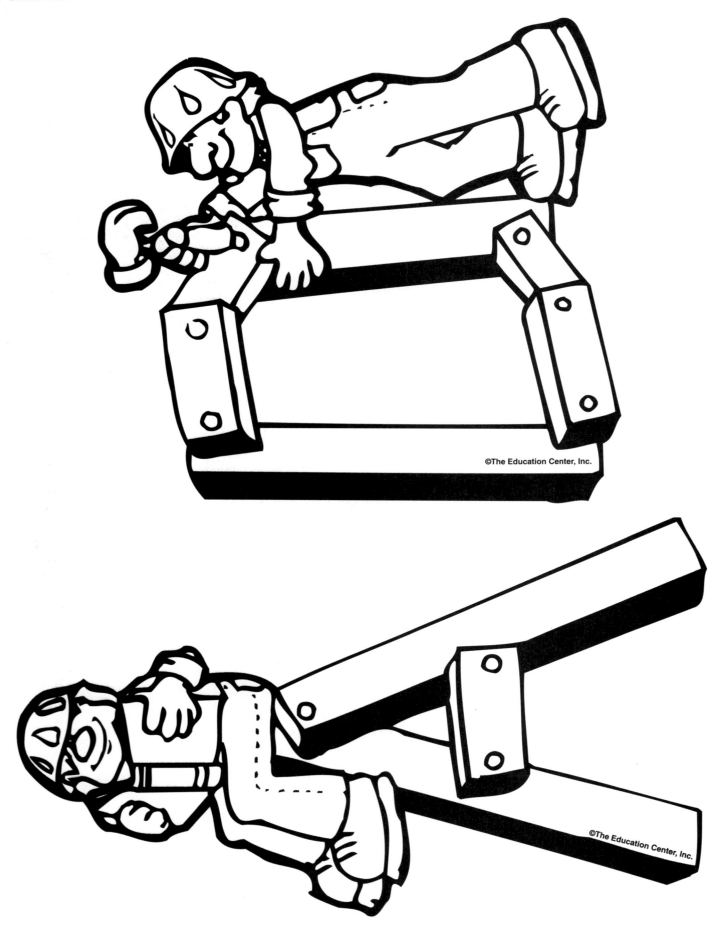

©The Education Center, Inc.

©The Education Center, Inc.

Enlarge and use with "Build A Better Future—READ!" on page 16.

Patterns

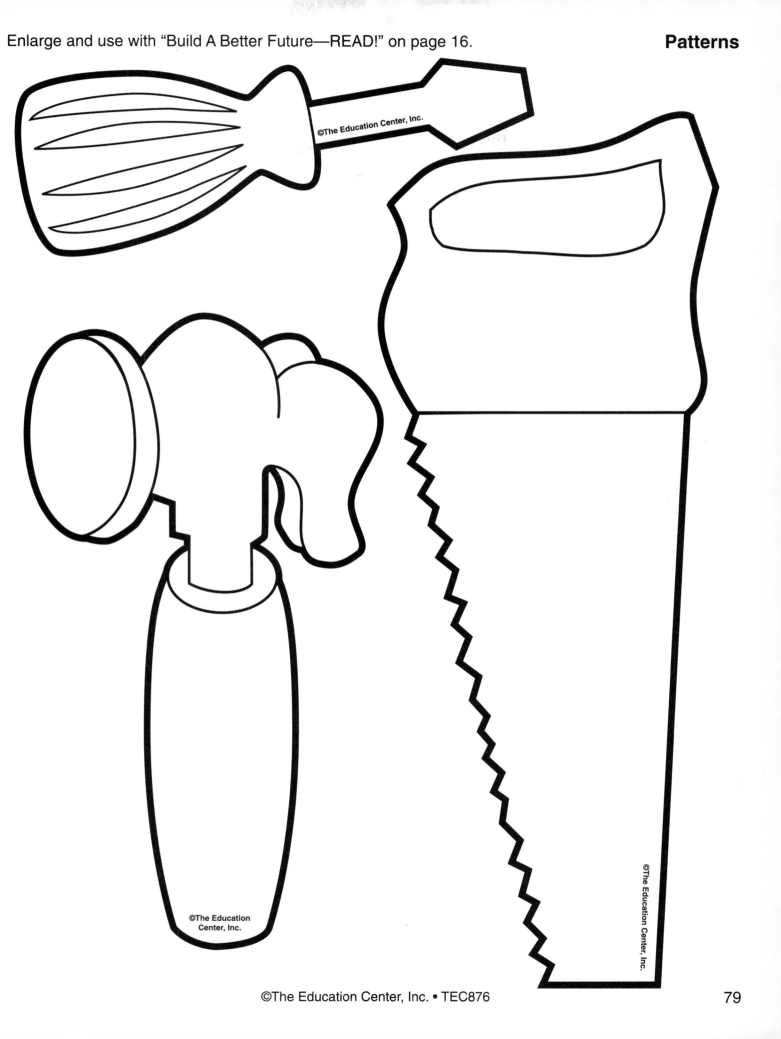

©The Education Center, Inc.

Enlarge and use with "Get Hooked On Books!" on page 16.

©The Education Center, Inc.

©The Education Center, Inc.

©The Education Center, Inc. • TEC876

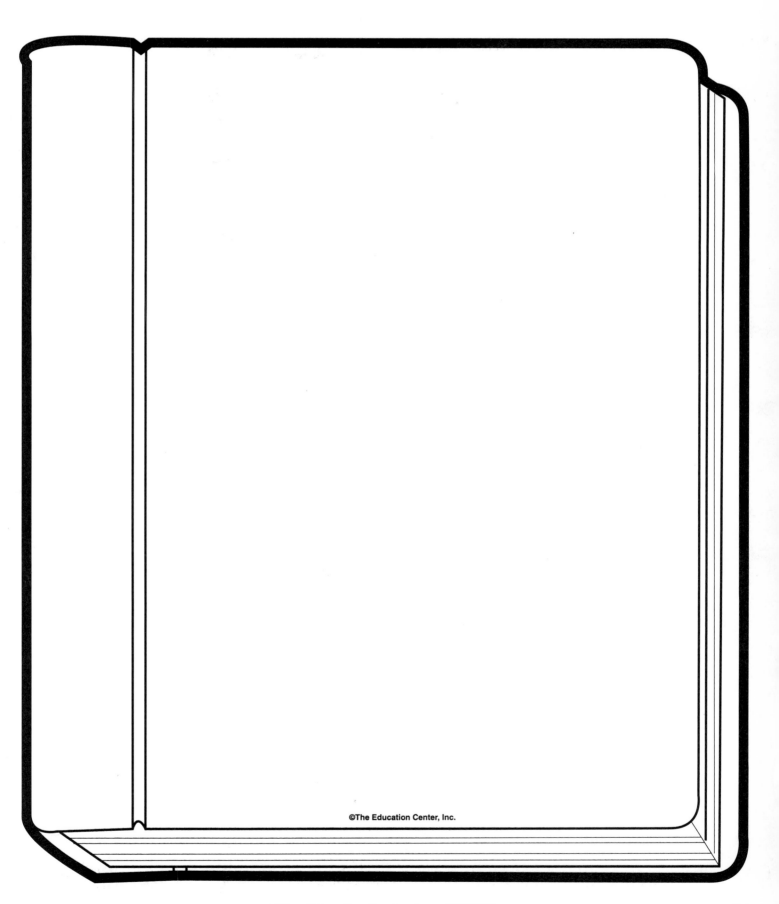

©The Education Center, Inc.

Bookmarks

Duplicate and use with "Get Hooked On Books!" on page 16.

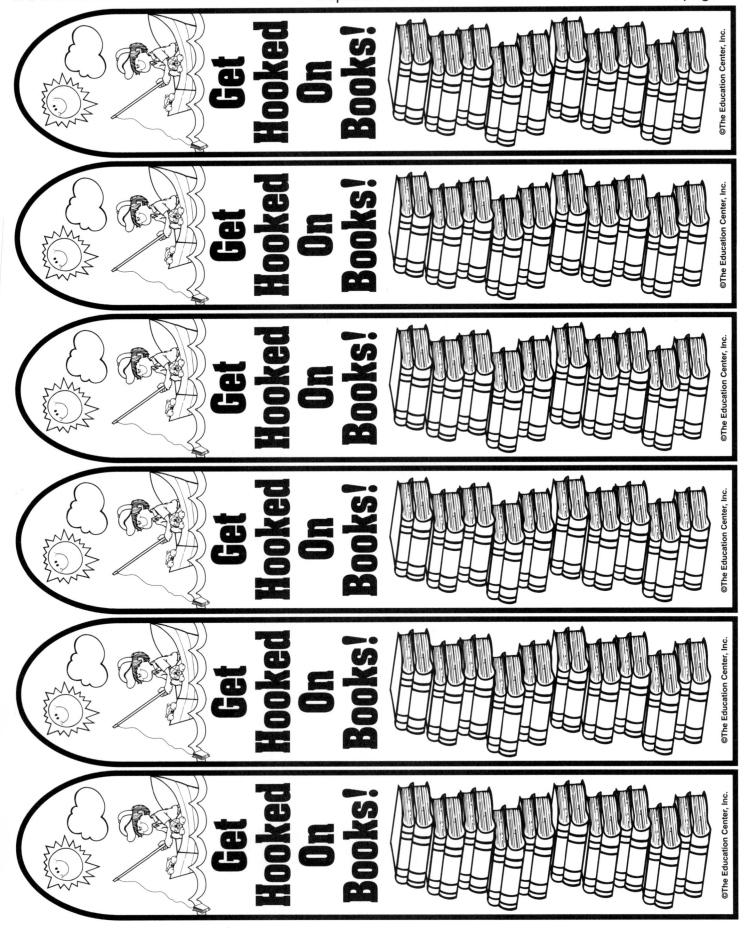

Get Hooked On Books!

©The Education Center, Inc.

Enlarge and use with "Reading Is Out Of This World!" on page 17.

Patterns

©The Education Center, Inc.

©The Education Center, Inc.

©The Education Center, Inc.

©The Education Center, Inc.

©The Education Center, Inc.

Pattern

Enlarge and use with "Reading Is Out Of This World!" on page 17.

84

Enlarge and use with "Reading Is Out Of This World!" on page 17.   **Pattern**

Pattern

Enlarge and use with "Reading Is Out Of This World!" on page 17.

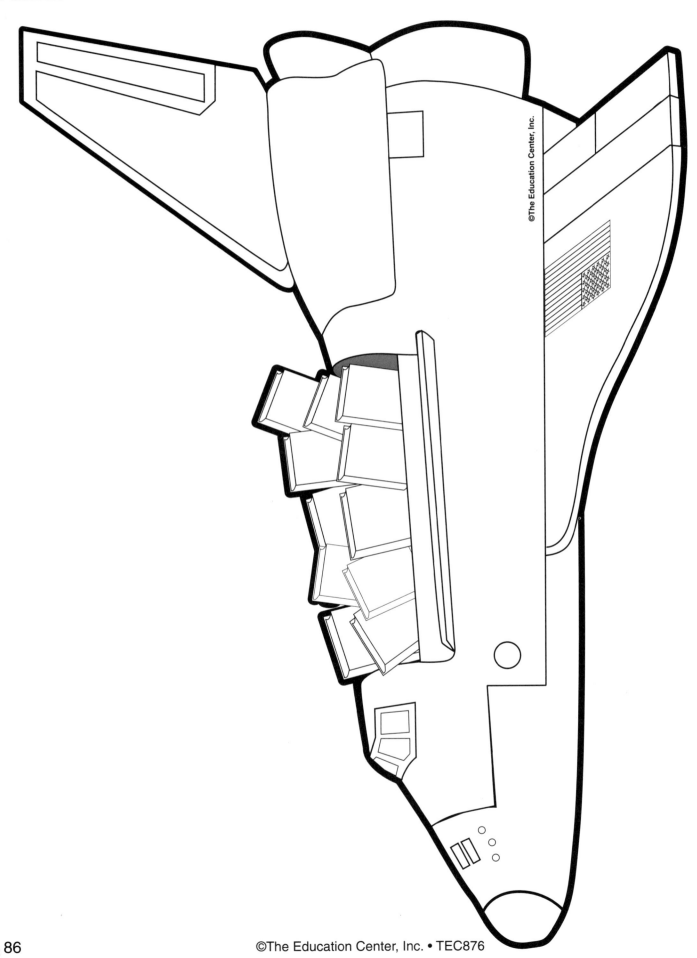

©The Education Center, Inc.

©The Education
Center, Inc.

Pattern

Enlarge and use with "Sharing The Harvest!" on page 18.

Patterns

Enlarge and use with "Gobble, Gobble, Gobble!" on page 19.

©The Education Center, Inc.

©The Education Center, Inc.

Pattern

Pattern

Enlarge and use with "Happy Thanksgiving!" on page 19.

92

Enlarge and use with "Happy Thanksgiving!" on page 19.

Pattern

Enlarge and use with "Happy Thanksgiving!" on page 19.

©The Education Center, Inc.

Enlarge and use with "Happy Thanksgiving!" on page 19.

©The Education Center, Inc.

©The Education Center, Inc.

©The Education Center, Inc.

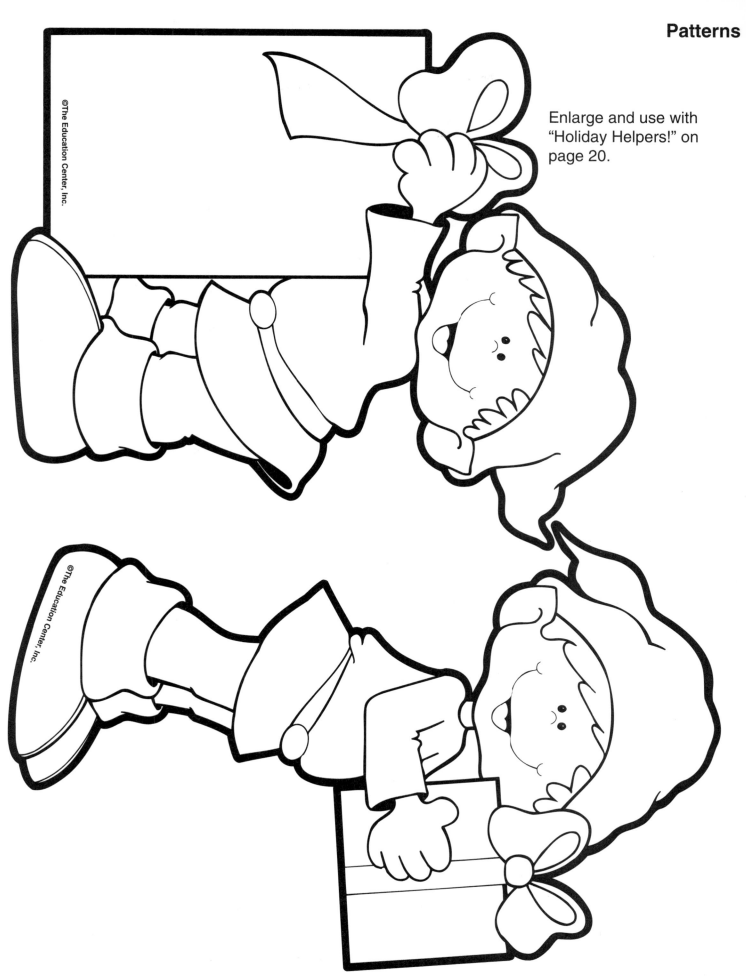

Enlarge and use with "Holiday Helpers!" on page 20.

Patterns

Enlarge and use with "Holiday Helpers!" on page 20.

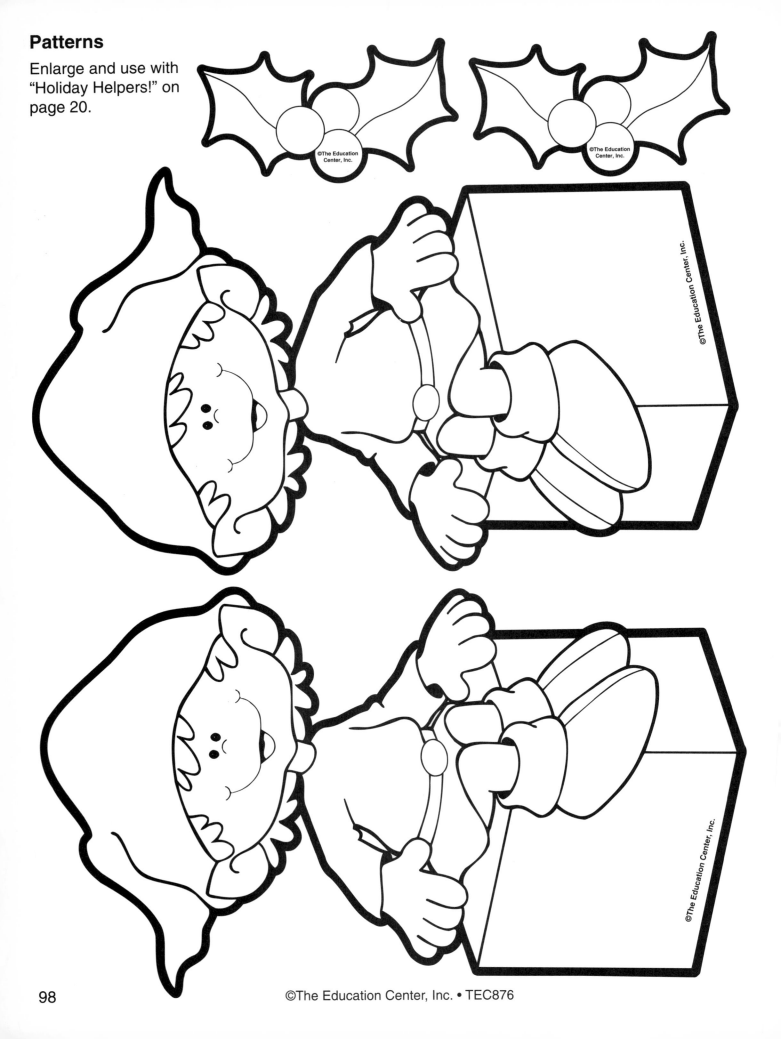

Enlarge and use with "Holiday Helpers!" on page 20.

Pattern

Enlarge and use with "Give A Holiday Hug!" on page 20.

©The Education Center, Inc.

Patterns

Patterns

Enlarge and use with "Peace On Earth" on page 21.

Scotland

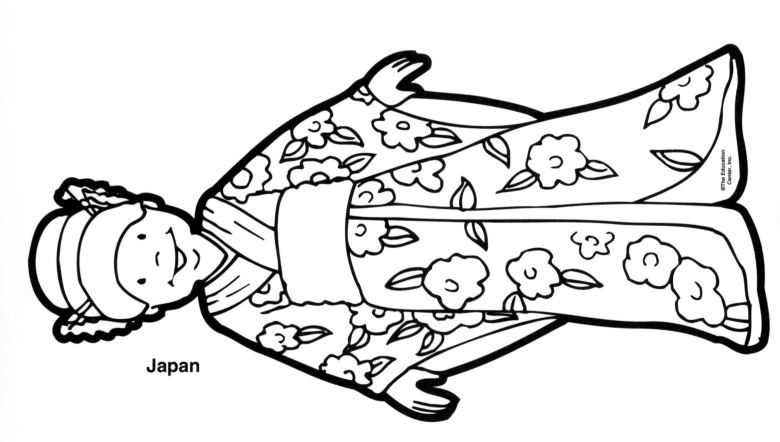

Japan

102 ©The Education Center, Inc. • TEC876

Enlarge and use with "Peace On Earth" on page 21.

Patterns

South Africa

Mexico

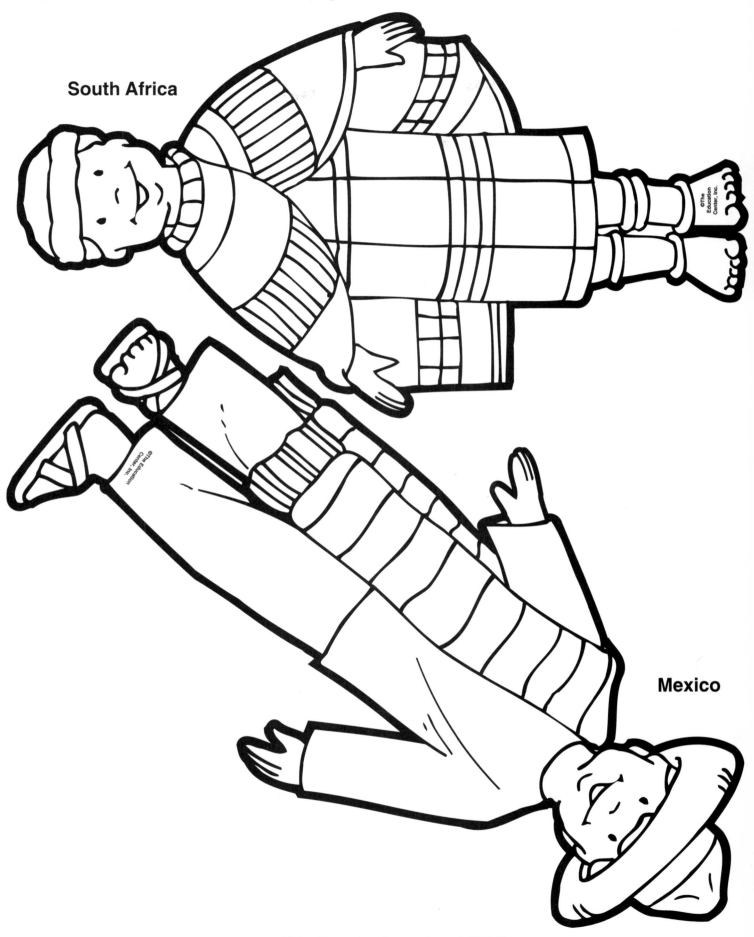

Enlarge and use with "Peace On Earth" on page 21.

The United States

The Ukraine

Senegal

©The Education Center, Inc.

Duplicate and use with "Peace On Earth" on page 21.

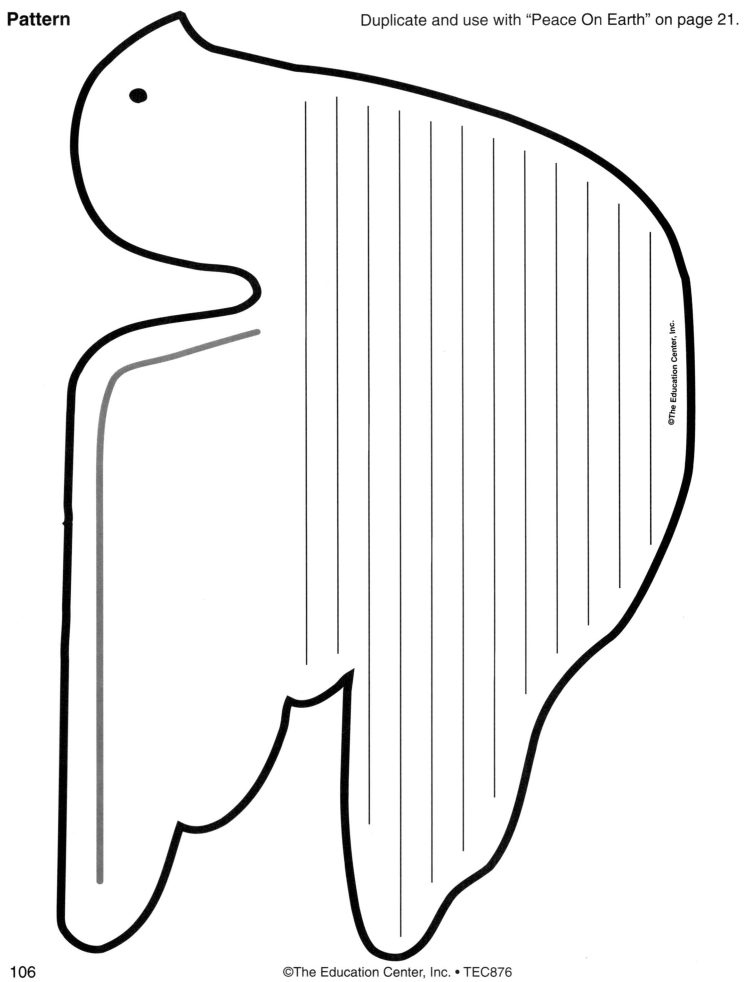

©The Education Center, Inc.

©The Education Center, Inc. • TEC876

Enlarge and use with Gingerbread door decorations on page 22.

Patterns

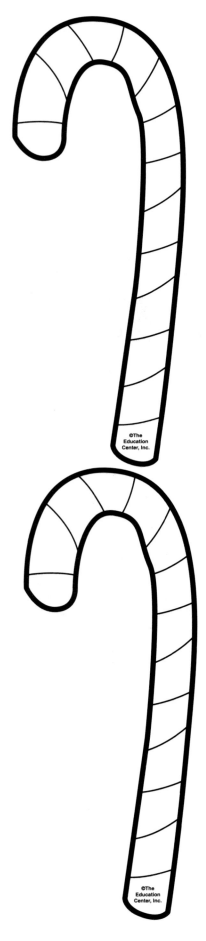

©The Education Center, Inc.

©The Education Center, Inc.

Duplicate and use with Gingerbread door decorations on page 22.

©The Education Center, Inc.

©The Education Center, Inc.

©The Education Center, Inc.

©The Education Center, Inc.

Duplicate and use with Gingerbread door decorations on page 22.

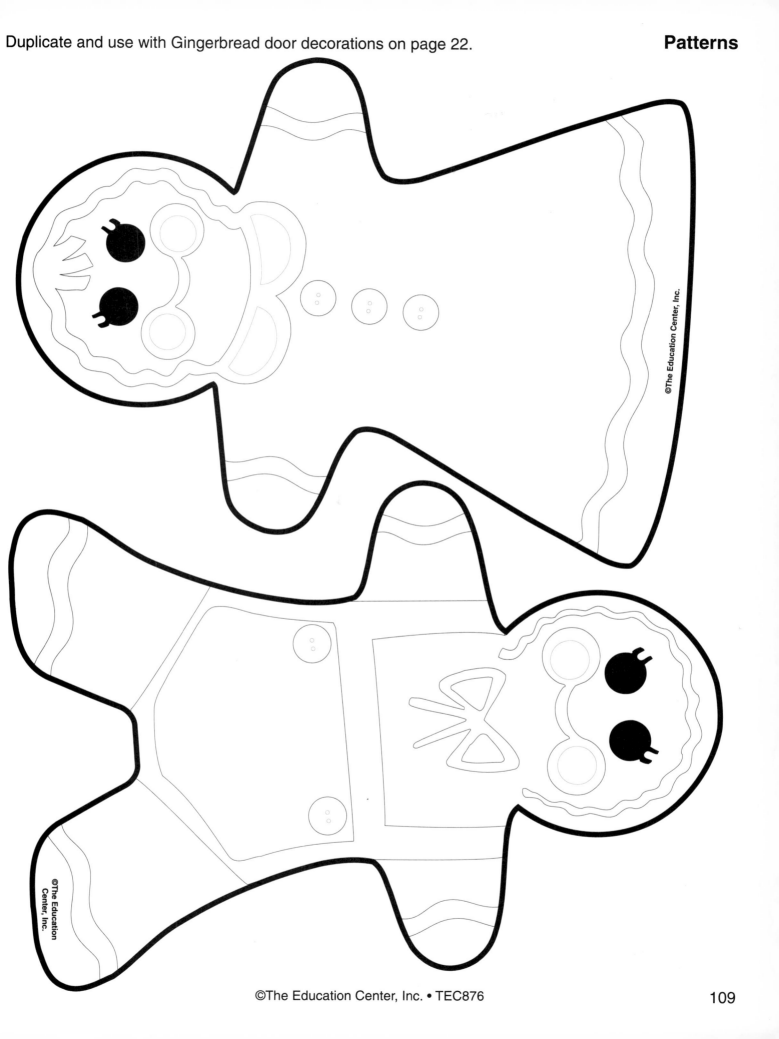

©The Education
Center, Inc.

©The Education Center, Inc. • TEC876

Enlarge and use with "A Fine-feathered Christmas!" on page 22.

Pattern

©The Education Center, Inc.

©The Education Center, Inc. • TEC876

Duplicate and use with "A Fine-feathered Christmas!" on page 22.

Patterns

©The Education Center, Inc.

©The Education Center, Inc.

©The Education Center, Inc.

©The Education Center, Inc.

©The Education Center, Inc.

©The Education Center, Inc.

Enlarge and use with "Put Your Best Foot Forward!" on page 24.

©The Education Center, Inc.

©The Education Center, Inc.

Enlarge and use with "Put Your Best Foot Forward!" on page 24.

Patterns

©The Education Center, Inc.

©The Education Center, Inc.

©The Education Center, Inc.

Enlarge and use with "Polar Pals" on page 24.

©The Education Center, Inc.

©The Education Center, Inc.

©The Education Center, Inc. • TEC876

Enlarge and use with "Polar Pals" on page 24.

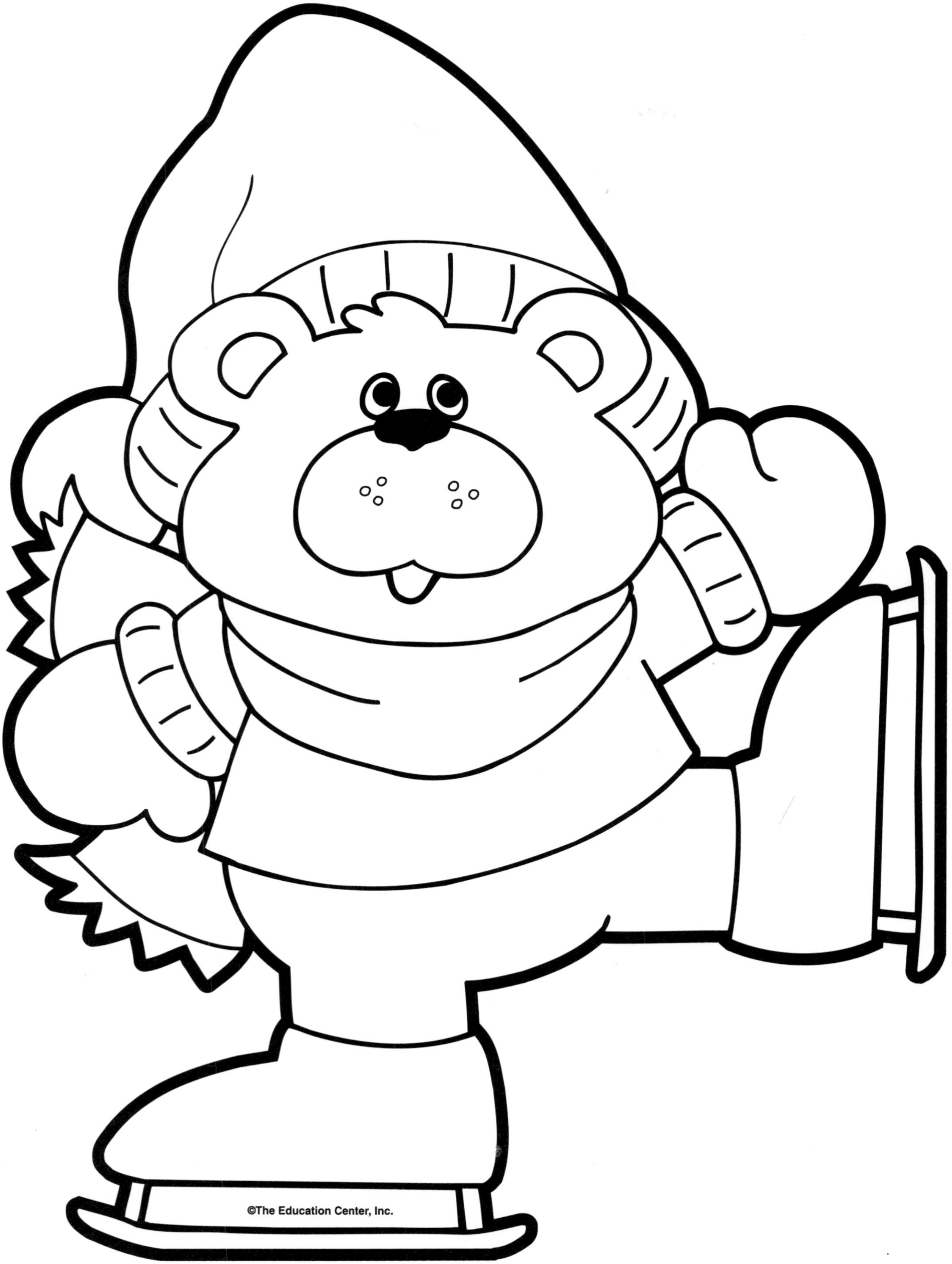
©The Education Center, Inc.

Pattern

Enlarge and use with "Winter Winners!" on page 25.

©The Education Center, Inc.

Pattern

Duplicate and use with "Winter Winners!" on page 25.

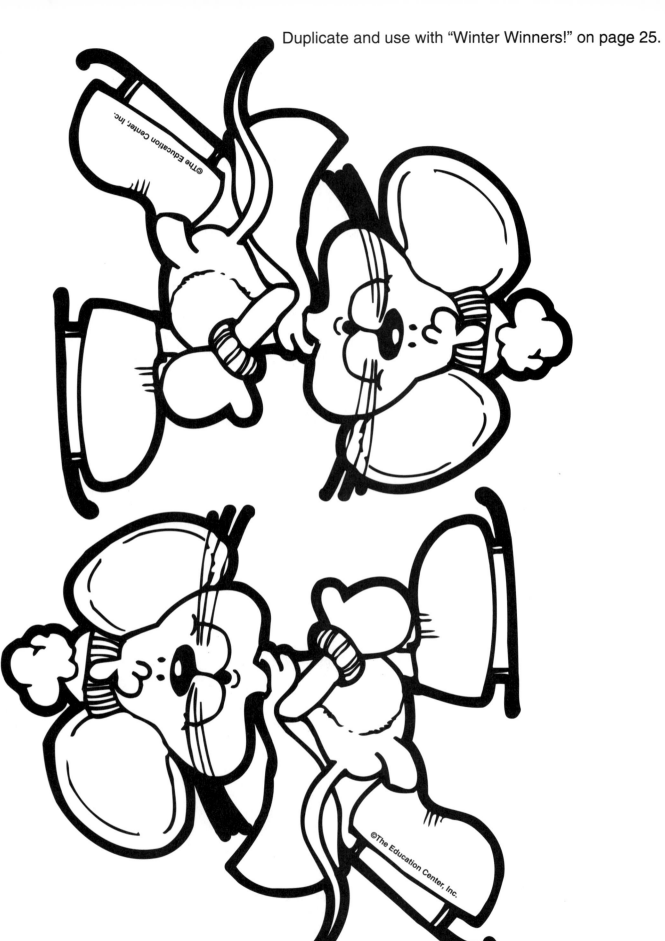

Enlarge and use with "Puppy Love" on page 26.

©The Education Center, Inc.

Enlarge and use with "Puppy Love" on page 26.

Patterns

©The Education Center, Inc.

Enlarge and use with "Head Over Heels!" on page 26.

©The Education Center, Inc.

©The Education Center, Inc.

©The Education Center, Inc.

Patterns

Pattern

Enlarge and use with "Be Mine Valentine" on page 27.

©The Education Center, Inc.

Pattern

Enlarge and use with "Be Mine Valentine" on page 27.

©The Education Center, Inc.

Enlarge and use with "We're Proud To Be Americans!" on page 28.

Pattern

Enlarge and use with "We're Proud To Be Americans!" on page 28.

©The Education Center, Inc.

©The Education Center, Inc. • TEC876

Patterns

Pattern

Enlarge and use with "We're Proud To Be Americans!" on page 28.

134

Patterns

Enlarge and use with "Happy Teeth!" on page 28.

©The Education Center, Inc.

©The Education Center, Inc.

©The Education Center, Inc. • TEC876

Enlarge and use with "The Wee People" on page 29.

Enlarge and use with "Leapin' Leprechauns!" on page 29.

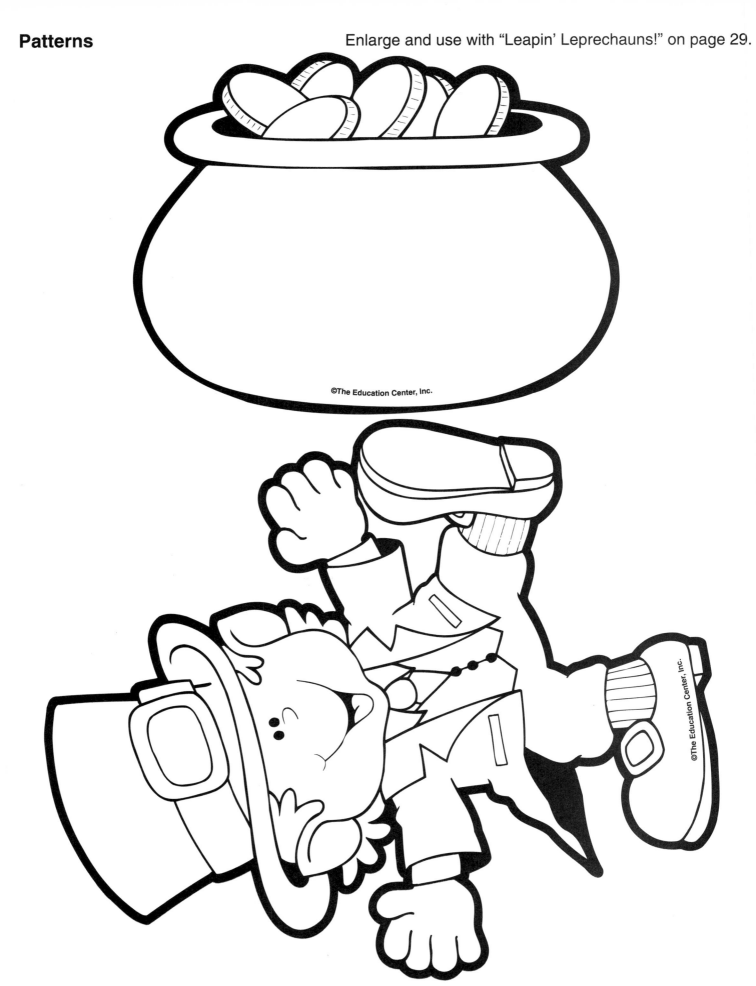

©The Education Center, Inc.

Enlarge and use with "Flying Facts" on page 30.

Patterns

Enlarge and use with "Flying Facts" on page 30.

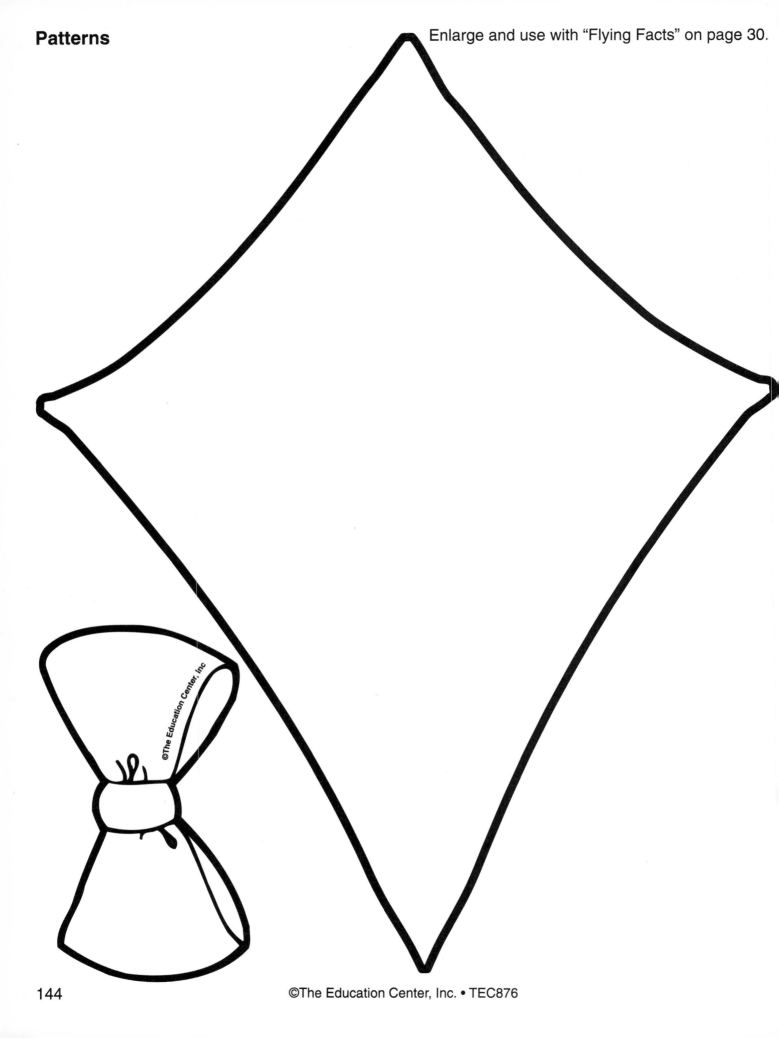

©The Education Center, Inc

©The Education Center, Inc. • TEC876

©The Education Center, Inc.

©The Education Center, Inc.

Enlarge and use with "Garden Bunnies" on page 32.

Patterns

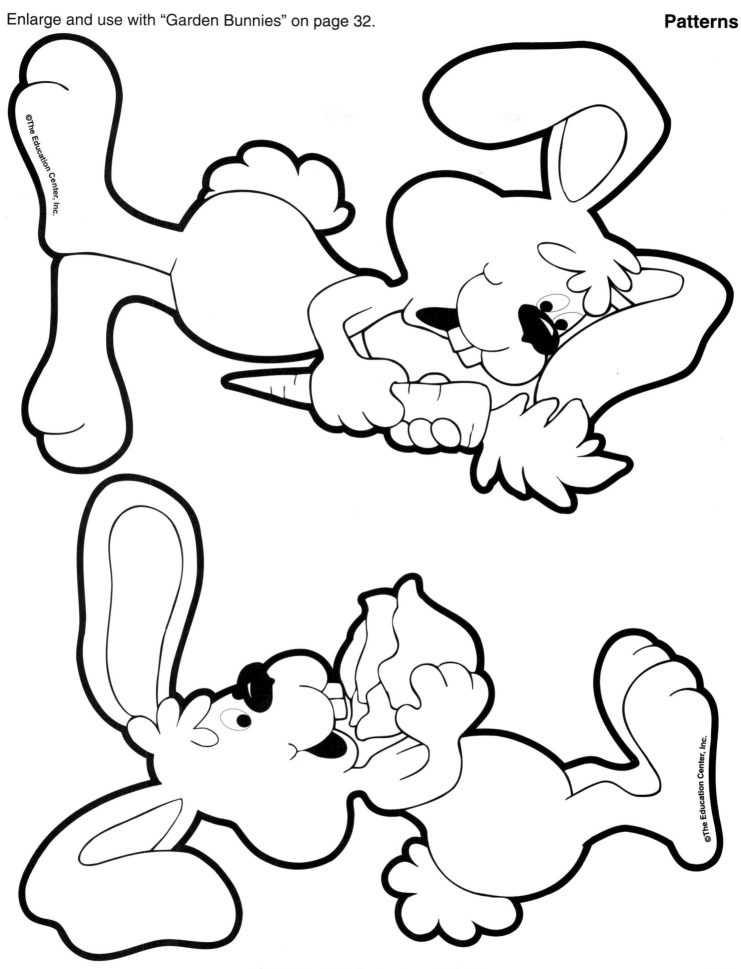

©The Education Center, Inc.

©The Education Center, Inc.

Patterns

Enlarge and use with "Garden Bunnies" on page 32.

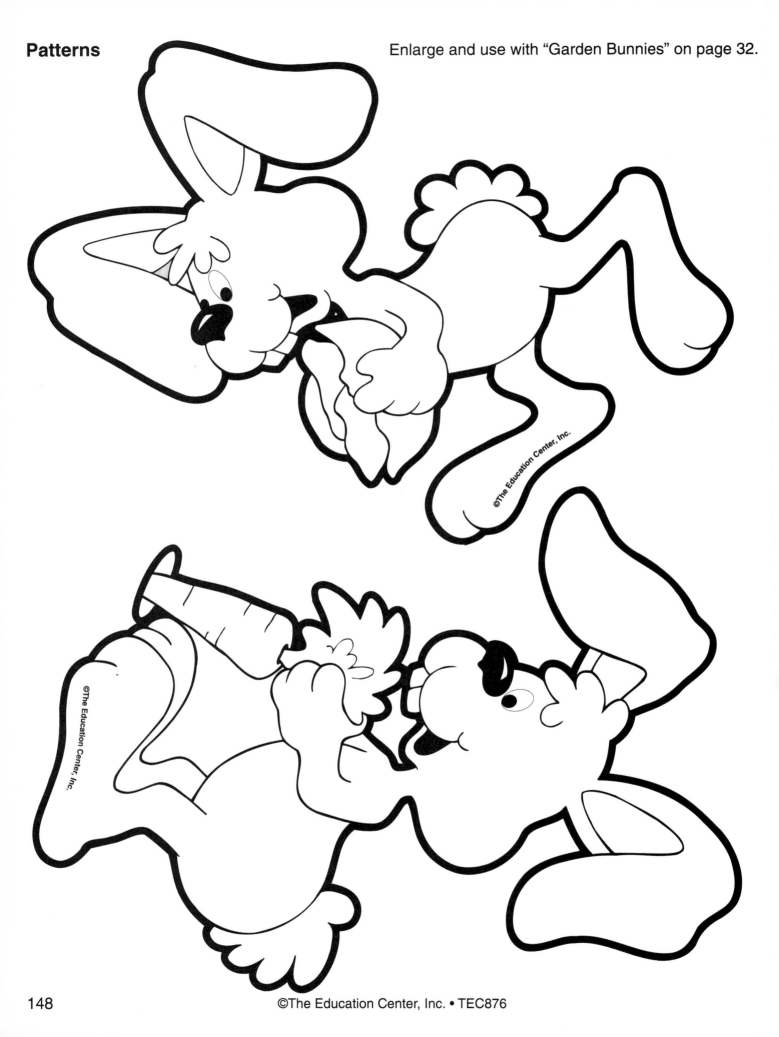

©The Education Center, Inc.

©The Education Center, Inc.

Enlarge and use with "Just Ducky" on page 33.

Pattern

Enlarge and use with "Just Hatched!" on page 34.

©The Education Center, Inc.

Enlarge and use with "Just Hatched!" on page 34.

Enlarge and use with "Paintbrush Bunnies" on page 34.

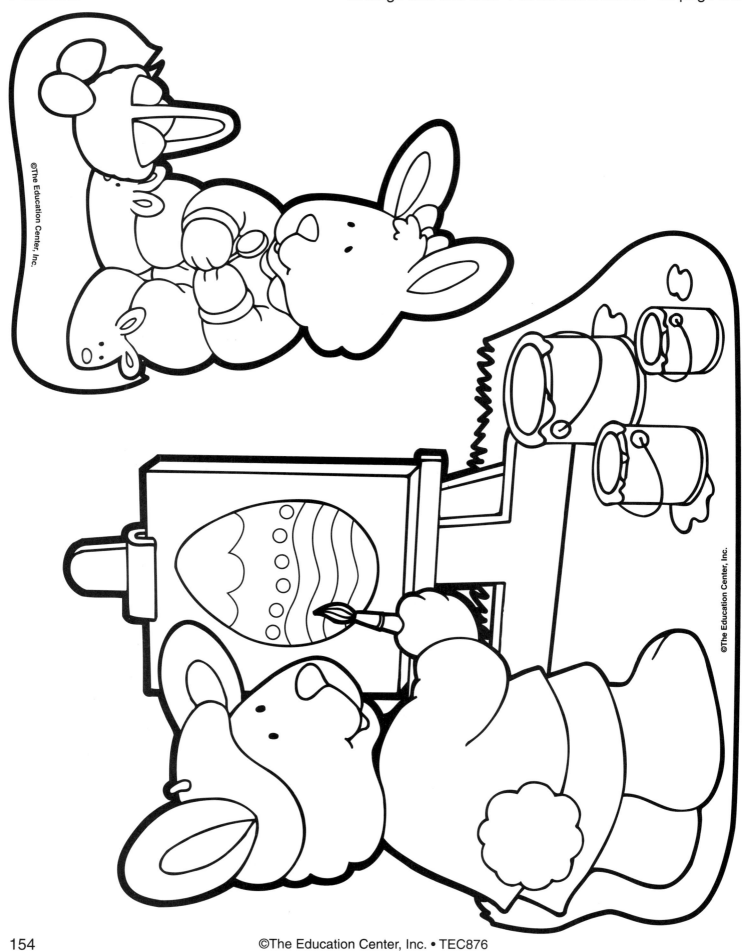

Patterns

Enlarge and use with "Paintbrush Bunnies" on page 34.

©The Education Center, Inc.

©The Education Center, Inc.

©The Education Center, Inc. • TEC876

Enlarge and use with "Hop, Hop, Hooray!" on page 35.

Pattern

Enlarge and use with "It's Been A Honey Of A Year!" on page 35.

©The Education Center, Inc.

Enlarge and use with "It's Been A Honey Of A Year!" on page 35. **Patterns**

Duplicate and use with "It's Been A Honey Of A Year!" on page 35.

©The Education Center, Inc.

©The Education Center, Inc.

©The Education Center, Inc. • TEC876

©The Education Center, Inc.

Enlarge and use with "What Time Is It?" on page 36.

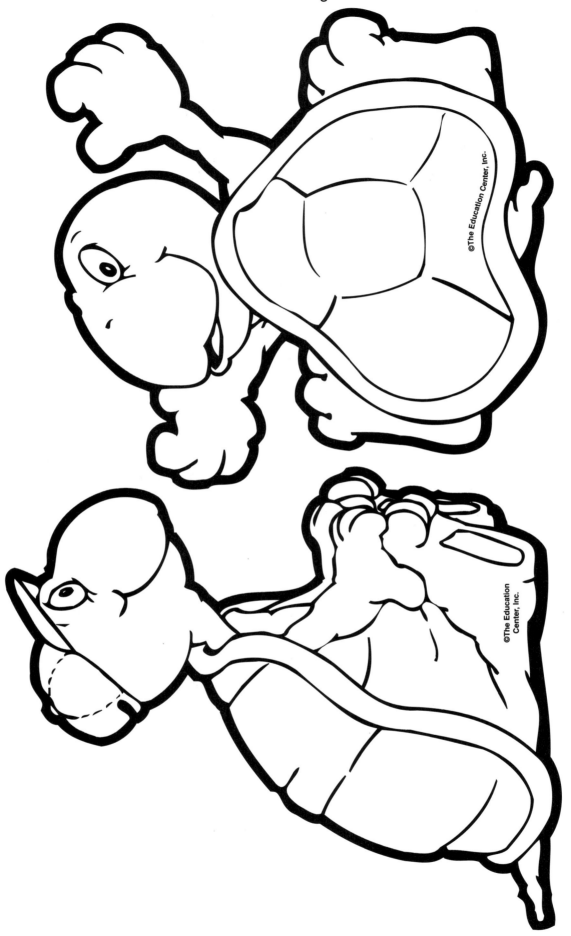

©The Education Center, Inc.

©The Education Center, Inc.

Patterns

Duplicate and use with "What Time Is It?" on page 36.

©The Education Center, Inc.

©The Education Center, Inc.

Enlarge and use with "Circus Bear Shapes" on page 36.

Pattern

©The Education Center, Inc.

Pattern

Enlarge and use with "Circus Bear Shapes" on page 36.

166

Enlarge and use with "Look What We've Cooked Up!" on page 37.

Pattern

Cut bottom of chef's apron as long as needed.

Patterns

Enlarge and use with "Look What We've Cooked Up!" on page 37.

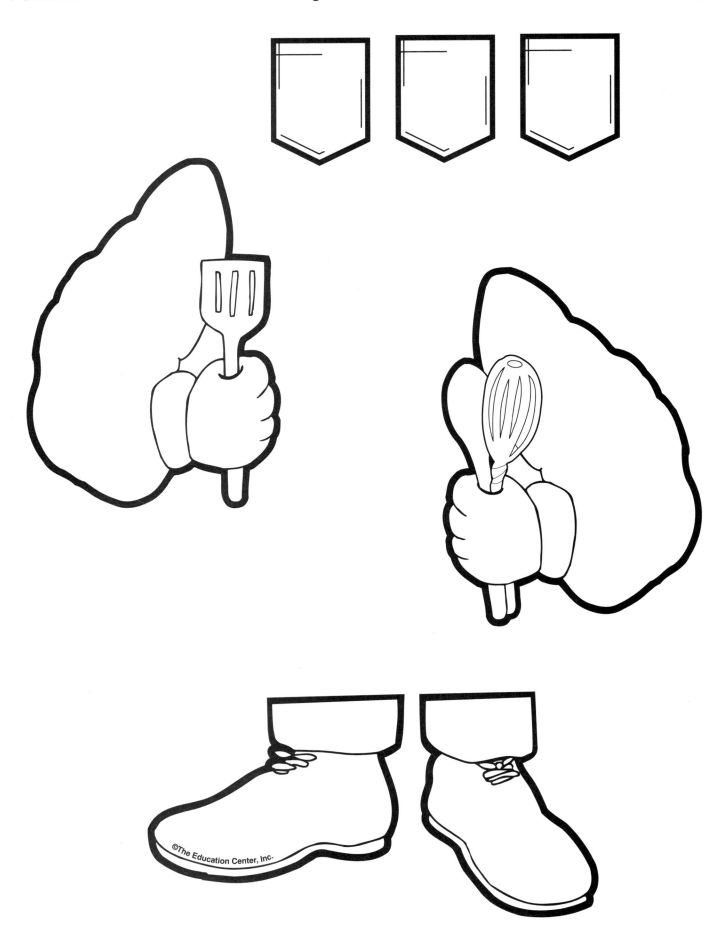

Pattern

Cardinal

Robin

Bluebird

Oriole

Blue Jay

Woodpecker

Chickadee

©The Education Center, Inc.

Patterns

Enlarge and use with "Birdbath Fun!" on page 38.

Chickadee

Robin

Bluebird

Oriole

Blue Jay

Woodpecker

©The Education Center, Inc.

170

©The Education Center, Inc.

Enlarge and use with "'Dino-mite' Work!" on page 38.

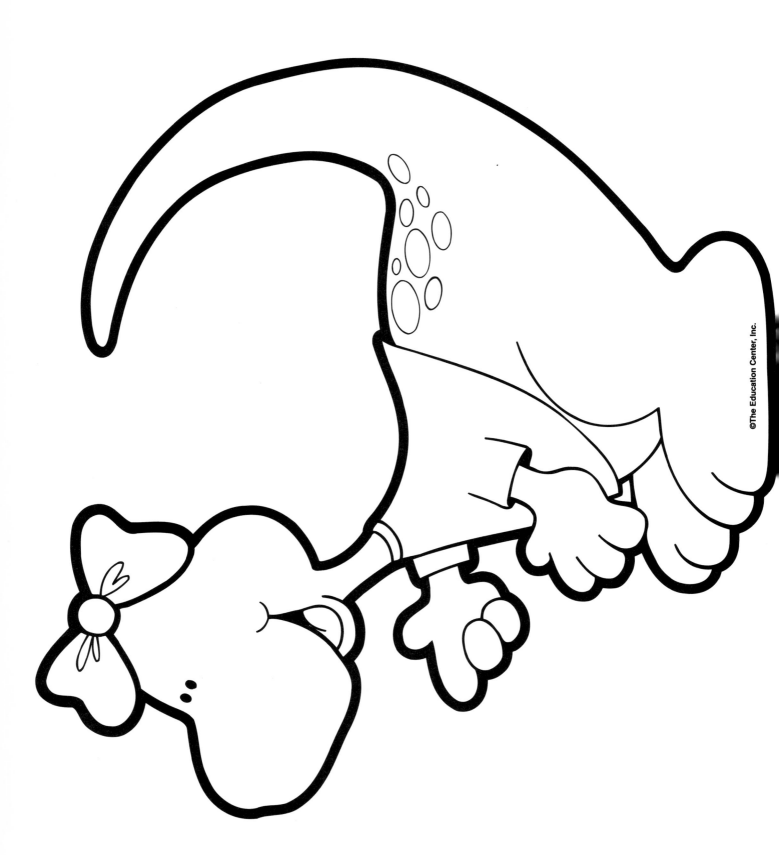

©The Education Center, Inc.

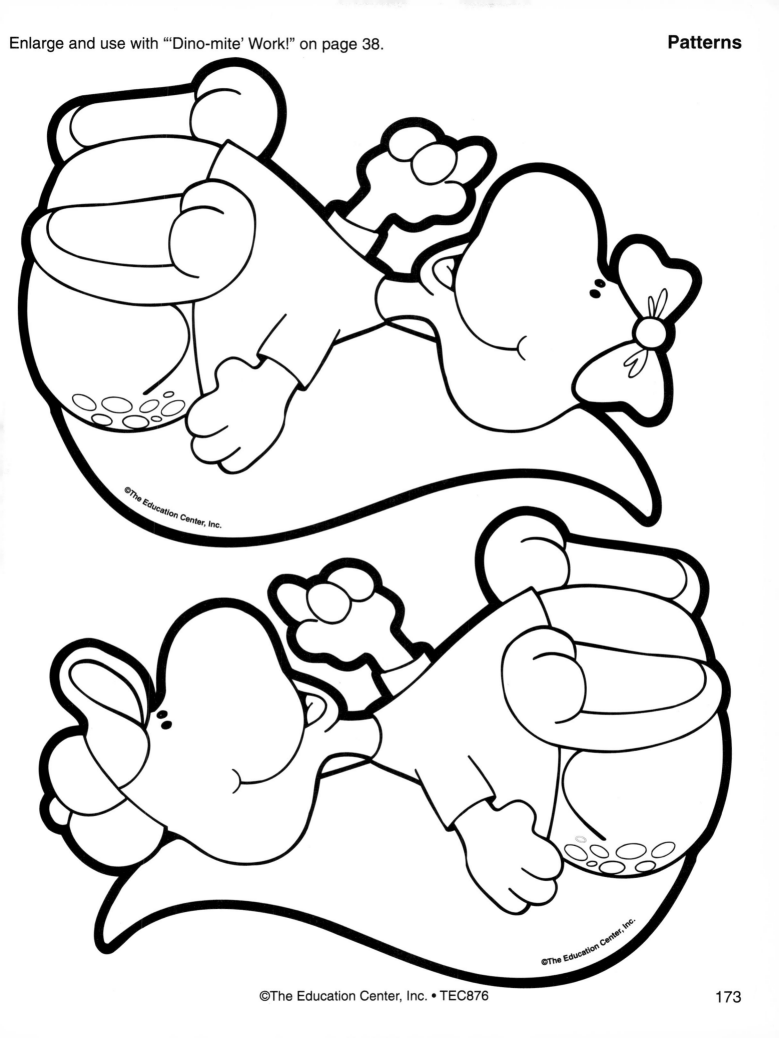

©The Education Center, Inc.

©The Education Center, Inc.

Enlarge and use with "Old MacDonald's Farm" on page 39.

©The Education
Center, Inc.

©The
Education
Center, Inc.

©The Education Center, Inc.

©The Education Center, Inc.

©The Education Center, Inc.

©The Education Center, Inc.

Patterns

Enlarge and use with "Under The Big Top!" on page 40.

©The Education Center, Inc.

©The Education Center, Inc.

177

Patterns

Enlarge and use with "Under The Big Top!" on page 40.

©The Education Center, Inc.

©The Education Center, Inc.

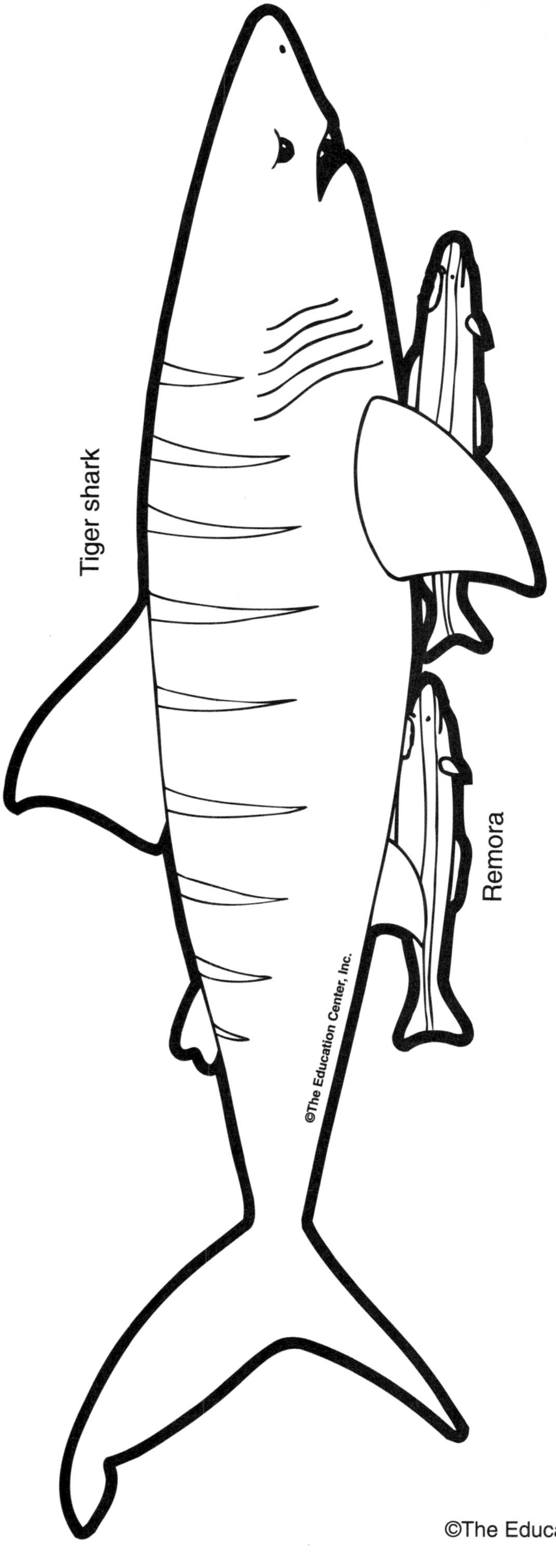

Patterns

Damselfish

Tiger shark

Remora

©The Education Center, Inc.

Butterfly fish

©The Education Center, Inc.

Enlarge and use with "The Ocean" on page 41.

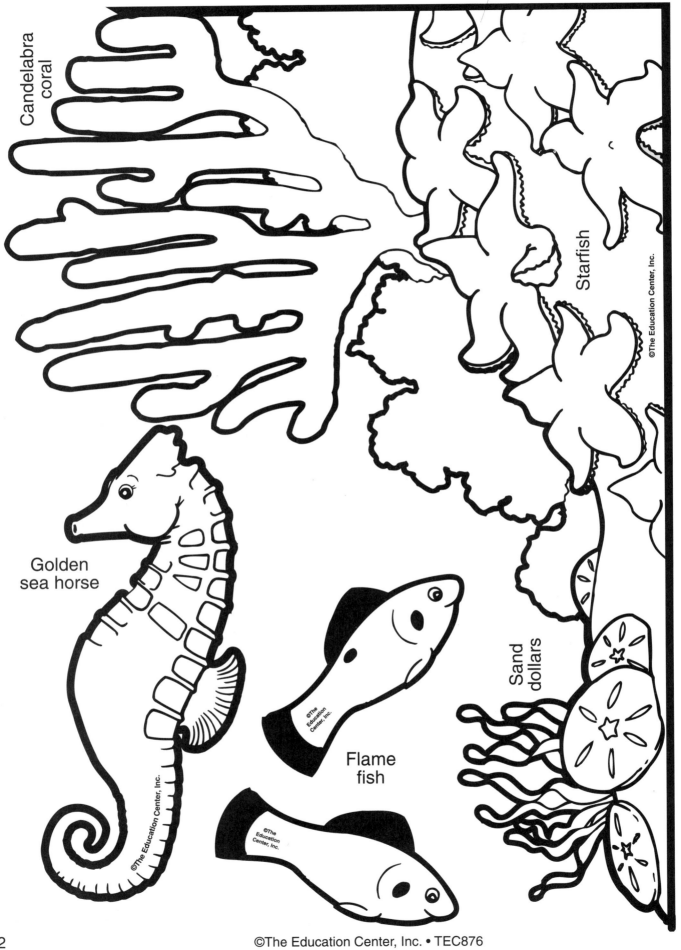

Candelabra coral

Starfish

Golden sea horse

Flame fish

Sand dollars

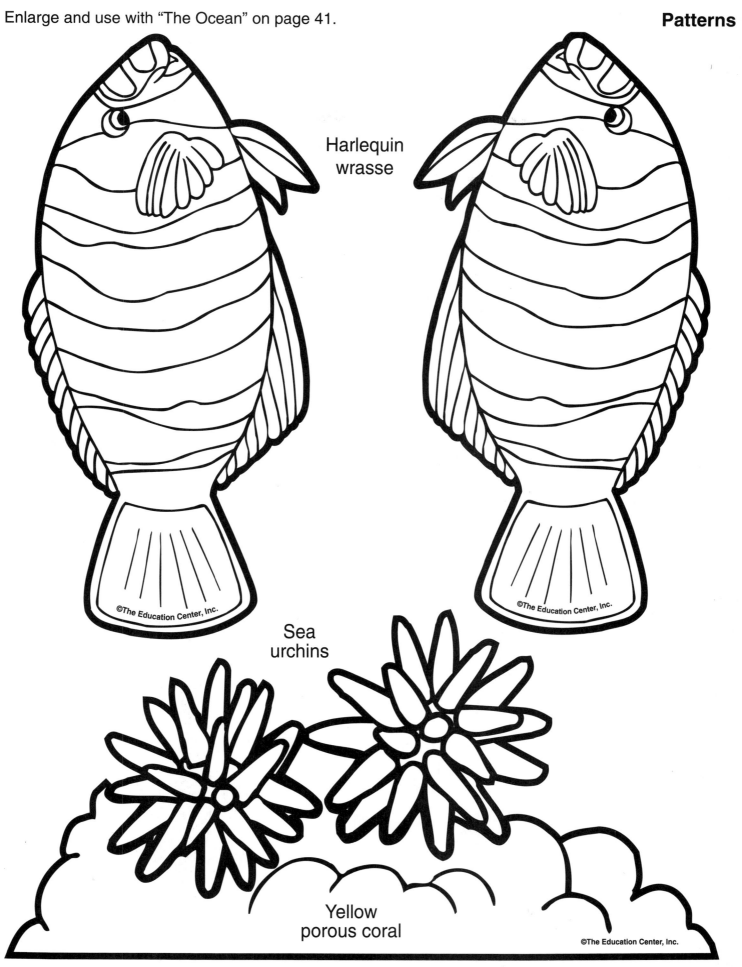

Harlequin
wrasse

Sea
urchins

Yellow
porous coral

©The Education Center, Inc.

Enlarge and use with "Pick A Posey" on page 42.

©The Education Center, Inc.

©The Education Center, Inc.

Pattern

Enlarge and use with "Whoo's Wise?" on page 42.

©The Education Center, Inc.

Patterns

Enlarge and use with "For Great 'Purr-formances'—Do Your Best!" on page 44. **Pattern**

©The Education Center, Inc.

©The
Education
Center, Inc.

Enlarge and use with "Give It Your Best Shot!" on page 44.

Patterns

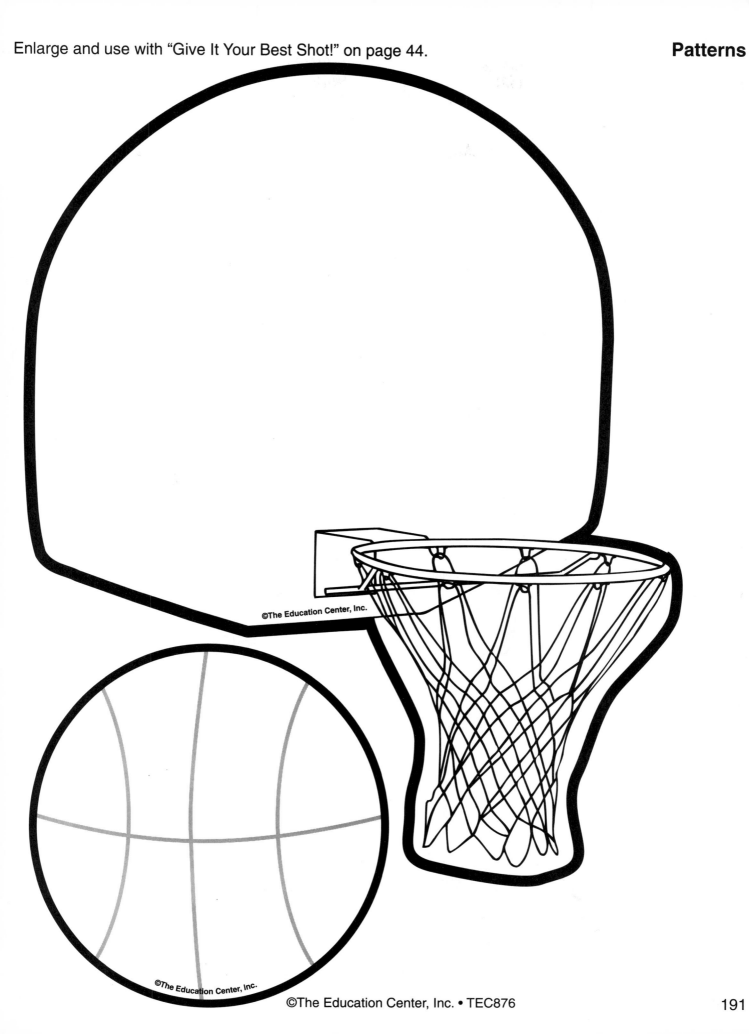

©The Education Center, Inc.

©The Education Center, Inc.

Pattern

Enlarge and use with "Give It Your Best Shot!" on page 44.

192